MUTINY MEMOIRS

MUTINY MEMOIRS

BEING

PERSONAL REMINISCENCES

OF THE

GREAT SEPOY REVOLT OF 1857

BY

COLONEL A. R. D. MACKENZIE, C.B.

GYAN

Published by

Gyan Publishing House
5, Ansari Road
Daryaganj, New Delhi-110002
Phone: 011-47034999, 9811692060
E-mail: books@gyanbooks.com

Distribution Network
gyanbooks.com
India, USA, Canada, UK, Australia

ISBN: 978-93-6208-079-0 (PB)
First Published, 1891

2nd Impression 2024

Printed at: Gyan Press, Delhi.

MUTINY MEMOIRS
Author: A. R. D. MACKENZIE

MUTINY MEMOIRS

THE CHUTTER MUNZIL, LUCKNOW, FROM THE RIVER.

MUTINY MEMOIRS

BEING

PERSONAL REMINISCENCES

OF THE

GREAT SEPOY REVOLT OF 1857

BY

COLONEL A. R. D. MACKENZIE, *C. B.*,

HONY. A.-D.-C. TO THE VICEROY

Forsan et hæc olim memenisse juvabit

1892

TO HIS EXCELLENCY THE MOST HONORABLE

The Marquess of Lansdowne,

G.M.S.I., G.C.M.G., G.M.I.E.,

VICEROY AND GOVERNOR-GENERAL OF INDIA,

THIS SHORT RECORD OF PERSONAL ADVENTURE

DURING THE GREAT INDIAN MUTINY OF

1857 IS, BY PERMISSION, AND

WITH PROFOUND RESPECT,

DEDICATED BY

The Author

PREFACE

THE reminiscences contained in the following pages were originally published in the columns of the PIONEER; *and it is with the kind permission of the Editor of that Journal that I am enabled to reissue them in the form of this little book.*

They do not pretend to any merit but that of truth. In that respect they may claim to present a record of actual events, and thus to bring before the Reader, however imperfectly, a rough sketch of the great Indian Mutiny such as it appeared to the eyes of a young Subaltern Officer of Native Cavalry, who had the good fortune to be engaged in its suppression.

I am indebted to the courtesy of the eminent Photographic Artists, Messrs. Bourne and Shepherd, for permission to copy the beautiful pictures which illustrate the text.

CONTENTS

MUTINY MEMOIRS.

I.

THE OUTBREAK.

IN jotting down the reminiscences and sketches contained in the following pages, my aim is to record simply and truthfully certain episodes of a stirring period of Indian military history.

Englishmen can never cease to be interested in the story of the great Sepoy Mutiny; and I trust that even so modest a contribution as mine to the narrative of some of its details may not be considered superfluous. Often have I been urged to give the semi-permanence of printer's ink to some story told over the walnuts and the wine; and at last I am tempted to take advantage of the enforced leisure which has been imposed on me by the recent regulations limiting tenure of regimental command, and placing me, with many other better men, unwillingly *en retraite*, while still in the prime of life and energy.

If I am compelled, in the course of these pages, to speak of myself and my own doings, I trust that I may be absolved from the imputation of being prompted by vainglorious motives; and that my excuse may be found in the evident impossibility of keeping the first personal pronoun out of a personal narrative. My having been mixed up in the events which I propose to describe is clearly an accident for which, though I may apologise, I am not responsible; and perhaps if I had not been engaged in them I should have known a good deal less about them. Whether that is an advantage, or the reverse, to a *raconteur*, is, of course, a matter of opinion. Certainly, a witness is much less hampered in his statements if he is not limited and bound down by the fact of his having been actually present at the scenes described in his evidence. His imaginative faculties are thereby quickened and enriched.

Hitherto, though often sorely tempted, I have refrained from publishing any account of those details of events during the Mutiny at which I was myself present; for, as will be seen, these details involve certain corrections in narratives which have been, for want of fuller information, accepted as complete. While perfectly true, in most points, so far as they have gone, they yet suffer from omissions which I am able to supply. The accuracy of my rectifications is, fortunately, capable of ample proof, since several very distinguished officers still survive who can vouch for it; and in most instances I am also in possession of conclusive contemporary documentary evidence.

It is not my intention to inflict on the reader my own views as to the origin of the Mutiny. Whether the *fons et origo mali* was deep-seated and of slow growth—whether it was due to political discontent at the overthrow of the great Mogal Empire, the annexation of Oudh, and the reduction of the King of Delhi to the position of a puppet of John Company Bahadur—or whether it arose simply from the excessive and pampered growth of the sepoy army, which, like the ass Jeshuron, waxed fat and kicked, is a question which has been often dealt with by abler pens than mine. It is, however, a significant fact that many clear-sighted men had, from time to time, issued notes of warning as to the likelihood of such a catastrophe.

When at length the threatened storm burst, my regiment, the late 3rd Bengal Light Cavalry, was one of those which broke into revolt at Meerut. In its ranks were ninety men armed with muzzle-loading carbines; and it was these carabineers who first set authority at defiance by refusing to use the cartridges supplied to them, on the ground that they suspected the grease used in lubricating them to have been composed of hog's lard. This pretext was, on the face of it, absurd; since, as a matter of fact, the cartridges had been made regimentally; and all the men perfectly well knew that so innocent a compound as bees' wax and clarified butter had been applied as a lubricant. The word had, however, been passed throughout the Bengal native army to make the cartridge question the test as to which was stronger—the native soldier or the Government. Every one remembers the mysterious "chuppatties" or flat wheaten cakes which, shortly before the Mutiny, were circulated from regiment to regiment. The message conveyed by them has never been fathomed by Englishmen; but there can be no doubt that they were in some way a signal, understood by the sepoys, of warning to be in readiness for coming events.

Colonel Carmichael Smith, Commanding the 3rd Light Cavalry, with a view to test the willingness or otherwise of the carabineers of his regiment to use the cartridges, held a special parade for the purpose on the 24th of April 1857; and, after an explanatory speech, pointing out to the men the groundlessness of their fears, ordered them to use the cartridges. Eighty-five of them refused to do so. A court of inquiry was subsequently held on their conduct, followed by the inevitable court-martial. Only one finding was possible; and the sentence pronounced on all the culprits was one of ten years' imprisonment. This, in the case of some of the younger soldiers, was reduced to five years by the confirming officer, General Hewett, Commanding the Meerut Division. On the morning of the 9th of May the whole garrison of Meerut paraded to hear the sentences read out; after which each convict was fitted with a pair of leg-irons, fitted there and then, on to his ankles by blacksmiths.

In sullen silence the two native infantry corps, the 11th and 20th, and my own regiment, which was dismounted on that occasion, witnessed the degrading punishment. It would have been madness for them then to have attempted a rescue; for they would have been swept off the face of the earth by the guns of the artillery and the rifles of Her Majesty's 60th Foot, not to speak of the swords of the 6th Dragoon Guards, the Carabineers, all of whom were provided with service ammunition, and were so placed as to have the native regiments at their mercy.

For more than an hour the troops stood motionless, their nerves at the highest tension, while the felon shackles were being methodically and of necessity slowly hammered on the ankles of the wretched criminals, each in turn loudly calling on his comrades for help, and abusing, in fierce language, now their Colonel, now the officers who composed the court-martial, now the Government. No response came from the ranks. The impressive ceremony was duly finished. The prisoners were taken charge of by the authorities of the jail and a guard of native infantry; and the troops marched back to quarters. For a few hours all was quiet. The snake of insubordination was, to all appearance, scotched, if not killed. Every one hoped that the stern lesson had been effectual; but a rough disillusion was in store for us.

On the evening of the next day, the memorable Sunday, 10th of May 1857, at the hour when better folk were on their way to church, I was quietly reading a book in my own bungalow when my bearer Sheodeen suddenly rushed into the room, exclaiming that a *hulla-goolla* (in our vernacular, a riot) was going on in the lines, that the sepoys had risen, and were murdering the *Sahib logue*. Not for an instant did I believe the latter part of his story, even though the rapid and frequent reports of fire-arms, which now broke the quiet of the Sabbath evening, made only too clear the truth of the first. The thought that flashed through my mind was that our men of the cavalry were attacking the native infantry in revenge for the sneers with which we all knew these others had freely, since the dunishment parade, lashed their submissive apathy in witnessing, without an attempt at rescue, the degradation of their comrades. Sooth to say—so strong is the tie of *camaraderie*—my sympathies were all in the wrong direction; and I would secretly have rejoiced to have seen the insult avenged. Hurriedly putting on my uniform and sword, I jumped on a horse, and galloped towards the regimental lines; but I had scarcely got out of the gate of my compound when I met the English Quartermaster-Sergeant of my regiment flying for his life on foot from his house in the lines.

"Oh God! Sir," he exclaimed, "the troopers are coming to cut us up." "Let us then stick together," I answered; "two are better than one." For a moment he hesitated. Then, looking back, the sight of a small cloud of dust rapidly approaching from the distance overcame his resolution, and he rushed through the gate into the grounds of my bungalow, and scaled the wall between them and those of the next house. Instantly a small mob of *budmashes*,* prominent among whom I recognised my own night watchman, attacked him. The chowkidar thrust at him with his spear as he was crossing the wall, and cut open his lips. To my joy he fired one barrel of a gun which he carried with him, and shot the brute dead. He then dropped on to the ground on the other side, and disappeared from view. Later on will be found his subsequent adventures: for I rejoice to say he escaped with his life.

At this moment an infantry sepoy, armed with a sword, made a sudden swoop with it at my head I had not drawn my sword, and had only time to dig a spur into my horse's flank and force him almost on to my enemy. This spoilt his stroke, and his tulwar fortunately missed its aim, and only cut my right shoulder cord. By this time I had pulled my weapon out of its scabbard, but the sepoy declined any further swordplay, and promptly climbed over a wall

---

* Rascals.

out of my reach. As I turned from him and looked down the road to the lines, I saw that it was full of cavalry troopers galloping towards me. Even then it did not occur to me that they could have any hostile intent towards myself. I shouted to them to halt. This they did, and surrounded me; and, before I knew what was happening, I found myself warding off, as well as I could, a fierce onslaught from many blades. A few moments would have sealed my fate, when, providentially, the late Lieutenant Craigie emerged from his gate a little further down the road and came straight to my help. This diversion saved me. The troopers scattered past us and made off towards the European lines. It was only too clear now that a mutiny, and that of the most serious kind, was in full swing. Our duty was plain, though very hard to perform, for at this moment Lieutenant Craigie's Wife and my Sister were on their way together in his carriage to the church, situated in the European lines, and our first natural impulse was to gallop after them. But they had started some little time previously, and we hoped that they had already reached their destination, and were in safety among the British troops. Military discipline sometimes tries a soldier to the utmost; and now we felt that Wife and Sister must be left in the hands of God, and that our place was among the mutineers on the parade-ground. Thither we went as fast as our horses could carry us, and found ourselves in a scene of the utmost uproar. Most of the men were already mounted, and were careering wildly about, shouting and brandishing their swords, firing carbines and pistols into the air, or forming themselves into excited groups. Others were hurriedly saddling their horses and joining their comrades in hot haste.

Nearly every British officer of the Regiment came to the ground, and used every effort of entreaty, and even menace, to restore order, but utterly without effect. To their credit be it said the men did not attack us, but warned us to be off, shouting that the Company's Raj was over for ever! Some even seemed to hesitate about joining the noisiest mutineers; and Craigie, observing this, was led to hope that they might be won over to our side. He was an excellent linguist and had great influence among them, and he eventually managed to get some forty or fifty troopers to listen to him and keep apart in a group. Suddenly a rumour reached us that the jail was being attacked and the prisoners released. Calling to the late Lieutenant Melville Clarke and myself to come with him, Craigie persuaded the group which he had assembled to follow him, and away we went towards the jail. The roads were full of excited natives who actually roared approbation as we rode through them, for they evidently did not distinguish in the dusk the British officers, and took the whole party for a band of mutineers. We three officers led, and as we neared the jail our pace increased, till from a smart trot we broke into a gallop. Already the sepoys and the mob had begun their destructive work. Clouds of smoke on all sides marked where houses had been set on fire. The telegraph lines were cut, and a slack wire, which I did not see as it swung across the road, caught me full on the chest, and bowled me over into the dust. Over my prostrate body poured the whole column of our followers, and I well remember my feelings as I looked up at the shining hoofs. Fortunately I was not hurt, and regaining my horse I remounted, and soon nearly overtook Craigie and Clarke, when I was horror-struck to see a palanquin gharry—a sort of box-shaped venetian-sided carriage—being dragged slowly onwards by its driverless horse, while beside it rode a trooper of the 3rd Cavalry, plunging his sword repeatedly through the open window into the body of its already dead occupant—an unfortunate European woman. But Nemesis was upon the murderer. In a moment Craigie had dealt him a swinging cut across the back of the neck, and Clarke had run him through the body. The wretch fell dead—the first sepoy victim at Meerut to the sword of the avenger of blood. All this passed in a second, and it was out of the power of our men to prevent it; but the fate of their comrade evidently greatly excited and angered them. Shouts of "*maro! maro!*" ("kill! kill!") began to be heard among them, and we all thought the end was approaching. However, none of the men attacked us, and in a few minutes we reached the jail, only to find that we were too late. The prisoners were already swarming out of it; their shackles were being knocked off by blacksmiths before our eyes; and the jail-guard of native infantry on our riding up to it answered our questions by firing at us, fortunately without hitting any of us. There was nothing to be done but to ride back to the cantonment.

No sooner had we turned our horses' heads than the full horror of what was taking place burst upon us. The whole cantonments seemed one mass of flames. If before we rode fast, now we flew; for the most urgent fears for the safety of those dear to us tortured us almost to madness. As we tore along Craigie allowed me to leave him and go in search of his Wife and my Sister, and to take any of the men who would go with me. I lifted my sword and shouted for volunteers to come to save my Sister, and some dozen of them galloped after me. As hard as our horses could gallop we tore along. Every house we passed was in flames, my own included, and my heart sank within me. Craigie's house alone was not burning when we reached it—a large double-storeyed building, in very extensive grounds, surrounded, as was then usual, by a mud wall. Here I found Mrs. Craigie and my Sister. They had never reached the church. Their coachman had turned back in terror of the mob. As they passed the bazar a soldier of the 6th Dragoon Guards rushed out of a bye-lane, pursued by a yelling crowd. The brave ladies, at the imminent risk of their own lives, stopped the carriage, took him in and drove off at full speed, followed for some distance by the blood-thirsty wretches who, being on foot, were soon left behind, not, however, till they had slashed with their tulwars in several places the hood of the carriage, in vain efforts to reach the inmates.

It is impossible to realise what terrors these ladies must have suffered till the moment of my arrival. Every minute they despaired of surviving to the next. All round them flames of burning houses and mobs of yelling demons! Not knowing whether the Husband and Brother were alive or dead—deserted apparently by God and man—hopeless of help,—they yet never despaired, nor lost their courage or presence of mind. Their first thought had been to find Craigie's weapons and place them where they would be ready to hand if he or I did ever come. Nothing had they overlooked. Three double-barrelled guns stood against the wall, with powder-flask and bullets and caps. They were not loaded, for the ladies did not know how to load them; and the unfortunate Carabineer was in a state of nervous collapse. Overjoyed, and thankful to Providence as I was to find them still alive and unhurt, I could not conceal from them that extreme danger was by no means over, and that they would yet have need of all their courage. The greatest risk I instinctively felt was from the uncertain temper of my men; and I determined on a desperate stroke. I therefore brought the ladies down to the door of the house, and calling to me the troopers commended their lives to their charge. It is impossible to understand the swift torrents of feeling that flood the hearts of Orientals in periods of intense excitement. Like madmen they threw themselves off their horses and prostrated themselves before the ladies, seizing their feet and placing them on their heads, as they vowed with tears and sobs to protect their lives with their own.

Greatly reassured by this burst of evidently genuine emotion, I now ordered the men to mount and patrol the grounds, while I took the ladies upstairs, and then loaded all the guns with ball. One of them I placed by itself against the wall. Long afterwards, in quiet England, my Sister, who still survives, told me that both she and Mrs. Craigie well understood the sacred use to which that gun was, in the last resort, devoted, and that the knowledge comforted and strengthened them.

Through the windows flashed brilliant light from the flaming houses on all sides. The hiss and crackle of the burning timbers—the yells of the mob—the frequent sharp reports of fire-arms—all formed a confused roar of sound, the horror of which might well have overpowered the nerves of the ladies; but I learned during that awful night the quiet heroism of which our gentle countrywomen are capable in the hour of need. As I stepped out on to the upper verandah I was seen by some of the mob who were wrecking the opposite house. "There is a feringi," they cried; "let us burn this big *kothi*" (house), and several of them ran forward with lighted brands to the boundary wall; but on seeing my gun levelled at them they thought better of it and recoiled. More than once this happened. It seemed only a matter of time before our house should be set on fire at one point or another. Fortunately I remembered the existence in the grounds of a small Hindu shrine, strongly built of masonry, on a high plinth, and with only one entrance, approached by a flight of stone or brick steps. If I could only get my charges and the guns and ammunition safely across the open space between us and that building, I felt sure of being able to hold out till help should come: for surely help would soon come! Were not the 6th Dragoon Guards, the 60th Rifles, and the Horse Artillery Batteries within a couple of miles?

At this juncture we were cheered by the arrival of Lieutenant Craigie, who, after I left him, had gone back to the parade-ground where the uproar was still at its height, the heroic efforts of the British officers to bring the men to reason being quite futile. At length, seeing the hopelessness of further endeavour, and finding the men getting more and more uncontrollable, they were compelled to retire and make for the European lines, carrying away with them the now for-ever disgraced standards of the regiment. One of them, the late Major Fairlie, also carried with him a bullet which was lodged in his saddle-tree. Craigie then made his way back to us at great risk of his life, accompanied by a few men who had never left him. He warmly approved of my plan; and, having explained it to the ladies, they quickly gathered together a few necessary articles of apparel, &c.; and each carrying her bundle, and concealed as far as possible under a covering of dark blanket, while Craigie and the Carabineer and I carried the guns and ammunition, we seized a favourable moment and ran rapidly across to our new stronghold.

Once there, we were safe from being burnt out, and indeed from successful attack of any kind by the cowardly crew with which we had to deal. The interior space was very small, probably about ten feet square. In front was the narrow doorway; and in the massive walls were slits like loopholes through which we could observe if any attempts were made to approach the place. Every now and then our troopers brought us news of what was going on. The night had not long closed in when they told us that apparently the whole body of mutineers, horse and foot, had marched away to Delhi. Their attack on the European lines, if they had made one, had clearly failed; and the only marauders remaining in Meerut were the butchers and other scum of the city and bazárs. Presently one of our men went over to the opposite house, which by this time was burnt nearly to the ground. He returned with awful news. He had found the dead body of its occupant, a lady, whose husband at the outbreak of the mutiny was absent in the European quarter. She had been most cruelly and brutally murdered, her unborn infant sharing her pitiable fate. He showed us, in confirmation of his story, a portion of her dress reeking with blood. Not far from us, another lady, while attempting to escape, disguised as an ayah, was recognised as a European, and murdered. Two veterinary-surgeons, attached to the regiment, had been killed—one of them with his wife—under circumstances of ghastly horror. They were both sick in bed with small-pox when the uproar of the mob startled them; and they came, in their night clothes, into the verandah, he carrying a gun loaded with shot, which he discharged at the crowd, only further enraging it. He was instantly shot dead. His wife met with a worse fate. The cowardly demons, afraid to touch her because of the danger of infection, threw lighted brands at her. Her dress caught fire; and she perished thus miserably. My own house-comrade, a fine young officer, had been mobbed on his way to church, and so hacked to pieces that but for his length--he was very tall—and the rags of his uniform which still clung to him, his remains would have been unrecognisable when they were subsequently recovered. A poor little girl, daughter of one of the British Non-Commissioned Officers of the regiment, had been slaughtered by a blow of a sword which cut her skull in two. Scenes like the above had been enacted all over Meerut; but I will spare the reader further details. If he is sickened by what I have already written, I can only say that mere generalities, however graphic, are insufficient to place before him a true picture of what English men, women, and children suffered at the hands of the mutineers, not only in Meerut, but almost everywhere through the North-West of India.

In these days of agitation for the repeal of the Arms Act, it is well to remind home-staying Englishmen of what once occurred, and what may again occur if a wave of political discontent or religious fanaticism should unhappily once more sweep over the "land of regrets."

Anxiously did we now listen for the rattle of horses' hoofs, the rumble of guns, or the tramp of feet coming to our help—but none came! Hour after hour passed—and still the mob were left undisturbed in their work of destruction and murder. We heard afterwards that a strong mounted party had been sent to clear the cantonments and rescue any survivors of the massacre; but—incredible to relate—it had been misled by the Staff Officer who was detailed to guide it, and never reached its intended destination. Among the troopers with us were one or two traitors, whose sole object in remaining was to undermine the loyalty of the rest. A young recuit who had, not long previously, passed through riding school in the same squad with myself, presently came to me as I was standing among a group of the men outside our stronghold (for Craigie and I now took it in turns to try and re-assure them by mixing with them), and warned me to be beware of the Havildar-Major, who had, he said, at that moment, been urging the others to kill me. It may be well imagined that I took very good care afterwards to keep a watchful eye on that Non-Commissioned Officer, and to let him see by a touch of my hand on the hilt of my sword that I was quite ready for any suspicious movement on his part. Soon afterwards he and a few others rode out of the gate, and we saw them no more. They had not long gone when a servant of Craigie's, a Hindu bearer, came up to us in great excitement with the news that a crowd of *budmashes* was coming in at the gate. He implored us to give him one of the guns, and let him go and fire at them. Whether wisely or not, we did so; and almost immediately afterwards we heard a report, followed by yells and groans. In a few moments the bearer returned, and gave us back the gun, saying that he had fired into "the brown" of the advancing mob, and brought one of them down, and the rest had fled.

It was now about midnight. The uproar was quieting down; and we determined on making our escape, if possible. So, with our own hands—the *syces* (grooms) having bolted—we harnessed Craigie's horses to his carriage; placed the ladies and the Carabineer inside with the three guns; made a native boy who usually rode postillion, and who fortunately had not gone off with the syces, mount one of the horses and set off, Craigie and I riding with drawn swords beside the carriage. This was a critical moment. A knot of the troopers, evidently wavering in their intentions, occupied the avenue before us, loudly talking and gesticulating. The postillion hesitated; but, on our threatening to run him through the body if he did not at once gallop on, he took heart of grace, lashed his horses, and in a moment we had charged through and scattered the impeding group, and were racing along the avenue at full speed over the body of the man who had been killed by the faithful bearer, and who was afterwards identified as a Musalman butcher, a class of men who were among the most blood-thirsty actors on that night. Turning out of the gate to our left we made along the road to the regimental parade-ground, from which a nearly unbroken plain stretched to the European lines. We found the plain deserted; and rapidly made our way till we reached a short length of straight road which ran to the stables of the Carabineers. At the far end of it we saw a light, which we rightly took to be a portfire. Making the postillion slacken speed, Craigie and I galloped forward, shouting "Friend! Friend!" at the utmost stretch of our lungs; and well was it we did so; for we found at a point where a bridge crossed a nullah a piquet with a gun trailed up the road; and the subaltern in command told us he was on the point of firing at our rapidly approaching group when our voices reached him. At last—with deep gratitude—we felt that our dear ones were once more safe among our own countrymen. The wife of a Sergeant of the Carabineers very kindly gave the ladies shelter for the rest of the night;

and Craigie and I shifted for ourselves, *al fresco.*

To revert to the adventures of the regimental Quartermaster-Sergeant after he left me. Covered with blood from the wound in his lip and carrying his gun in one hand and his sword in the other, he presented a sufficiently startling spectacle as he burst into a room of a neighbouring bungalow occupied by two young officers, and warned them—still unconscious—of what was taking place. Not a moment did they lose in buckling on their swords and rushing to the stables. As they did so they saw one of their own syces running away with a saddle on his head. They could only find two other saddles; but fortunately bridles for three horses were hanging on their usual pegs. Rapidly slipping them on, they mounted, giving the Sergeant a bare-backed animal, and they made for a gate. It was blocked by mutineers. They turned to the other: that also was blocked. Their lives seemed lost, when one of their servants, a sweeper, the lowest and most despised caste of Indian domestics, heedless of the certainty that his own life would be sacrificed to the fury of the mob disappointed of its prey, implored them to follow him. Running before them he led them to the back of the out-houses, and showed them a gap in the "compound"* wall which the servants had made for their own convenience. Through this gap they filed, and galloped off, escaping the hurried shots which were fired after them, and eventually reaching in safety the barracks of the 60th Rifles. The sweeper fell a victim to the rage of the pursuers. He was hacked to pieces. No more beautiful deed ever brightened the dark days of the "'57" than the self-sacrifice of this obscure and nameless hero.

---

* The name given to the enclosed grounds of a house in the North-Western Provinces.

II.

SKIRMISHING.

BEFORE continuing my narrative, I wish to draw particular attention to a circumstance which, so far as I know, has been overlooked by every historian of the Mutiny. This is the fact that as I was at the time informed, the military authorities, in view of the lengthening days and the increasing heat of the season, had caused, on May 10th, 1857, the evening church parade to take place half an hour later than formerly. In my firm belief, this change saved us from an awful catastrophe. In those days British troops attended divine service practically unarmed, for they did not take with them their rifles or carbines and ammunition. Their only weapons were their side-arms. The mutineers were, of course, unaware of this change. They broke into revolt half an hour too soon. Had they waited till the 60th Rifles were securely gathered into the church, what could have prevented them from overpowering the small guards over the rifles and the guns, and utterly destroying the defenceless crowd of soldiers penned, like sheep, within four walls. Providence befriended us. When the first scouts of the cavalry came galloping down to the European lines, they found the white soldiers falling into their places on parade. Once the alarm was given, all attempt at surprise was out of the question, and the hope of achieving an easy massacre was changed into fear of the awful retribution which they thought the European troops, now on the alert, would not fail speedily to exact. This fear altered all their plans, and hastened their flight to Delhi, so graphically described by Sir John Kaye; but, alas! no swift retribution followed.

The European troops, 1,500 strong, were paralysed by the irresolution of their chief. Had the gallant Hearsey or Sidney Cotton occupied Hewett's place at Meerut, it is safe to say that, in spite of the wings which fear lent to the mutineers on their flight to

Delhi, few of them would ever have reached that haven of their hopes. The shrapnel of the artillery and the swords of the Carabineers would have annihilated them. It is true that Generals Hewett and Archdale Wilson, late in the evening, moved the troops over the open plain of the infantry parade-ground and that they caused a few rounds to be fired, in the dark, at some belated stragglers of the cavalry, which said rounds, by the way, nearly killed an officer, Lieutenant Galloway, of my regiment, who had taken refuge in an out-house in the line of fire; but General Hewett, instead of even then detaching the Carabineers and a battery of horse artillery in pursuit of the flying mutineers, acted on the ill-starred advice of his Brigadier to withdraw the whole force to the European lines. No greater mistake from any point of view was ever committed.

There can be no doubt that the offer of Captain Rosser, of the 6th Dragoon Guards, to take a squadron and a couple of guns in pursuit, was really made and declined; for it was well known and much discussed at the time. It is true that intimation of this offer never reached the Colonel Commanding the Regiment; but it is equally certain that somebody blundered in not taking immediate steps to bring it to the notice of Colonel Custance. The prompt punishment which even such a small body could have inflicted would have been of the utmost value as a lesson both to the rebels and to the faint-hearted among ourselves; but the opportunity was wilfully thrown away; and the magnificent brigade of British troops of all arms, which afterwards covered itself with glory at the Hindun Nuddee, at Delhi, at Lucknow, and wherever its members met the enemy, was marched back to Meerut, and condemned for a period to the humiliating *rôle* of passive inaction.

Difficult as it is to understand, and impossible to excuse the motives which paralysed the nerves of General Hewett, it can only be hoped that all our officers have laid to heart the lesson so frequently learned in the great school of the Sepoy Mutiny that, in dealing with an Oriental enemy, *l'audace! et toujours l'audace* is not only the most soldierlike but the surest road to success. "Strike promptly and strike hard" should be their motto. Over and over again have small bodies of Englishmen, under the most desperate circumstances, and against the most fearful odds, by acting on this maxim, "plucked the flower safely from the nettle danger." When the day comes, as come it will, that we Englishmen will once more have to fight for the preservation of our Indian Empire, the issue will only be doubtful if timid and irresolute counsels prevent us from putting forth the whole of our strength at the first serious symptoms of internal disaffection or external menace.

During the next few days the Meerut garrison lay inert. Far from undertaking any distant reconnaisances or making any active efforts to restore to quiet the surrounding districts, not even was punishment inflicted on the city or the bazars, which had poured forth their swarms of murderers and robbers on the night of the 10th. A few individual marauders were, it is true, caught and hanged; but there retributive measures ceased. Native houses, choked with plunder, were left unsearched, and their occupants were allowed unmolested to swagger about in the sight of all men, and to boast among themselves of the shame and havoc they had wrought on the "Feringhi."

Our women and children and unarmed civilian refugees were given shelter in the "Dumdama," an often-described walled enclosure. The Generals and their staffs and many other officers took refuge in a barrack, over which a guard was duly mounted. Piquets, inlying and outlying, were told off; and every precaution was taken to prevent the cantonments being rushed by the "budmashes" of the "Burra Bazar" or the Goojars of the neighbouring villages!

As a comic element is never absent from the most tragic events, I may interpolate here a little story *anent* Colonel

Blank. That gallant officer rejoiced in a long and scanty moustache, which up to the moment of the Mutiny had retained the glossy black of youth. A few days afterwards, an officer who met me asked me if I had observed the terrible effect which late events had evidently wrought on the Colonel. "Poor fellow!" said he, "his hair has turned perfectly white!" My irreverent laughter amazed and shocked him. He little knew that the blanching of the old gentleman's moustache was due to his not having had the time or the presence of mind to bring with him in his hurried flight from the mutineers his trusty bottle of hair-dye.

A very few nights after the Generals and other officers had taken up their quarters in the barrack already mentioned, they suffered from a scare which, if it did not whiten their hair, might easily have proved a very serious matter to its innocent cause. This was how it happened. It must be premised that a row of beds lined each wall of the long barrack-room, each bed containing a

General, a staff, or at the least a field officer, every one of whom reposed his head on a pillow under which lay a revolver, while his sword was either resting on a chair beside him or hanging on the wall. Outside was a guard of British soldiers, and in the immediate vicinity were some fifteen or sixteen hundred more. Altogether as secure and well-guarded a dormitory as it is possible to conceive, and one in which the most timid and nerve-shaken creature might placidly entrust himself to the arms of Morpheus. Not so, thought one of its warrior occupants. Were there not three Hindu punkah-coolies in the verandah, and were not all their lives at the mercy of these miscreants? It behoved one at least to remain on the alert, and, with a watchful eye on the coolie toiling at the punkah rope at one end of the room, to safeguard the lives of all the careless sleepers. He should be that one! So, ostentatiously snoring, and pretending to be wrapped in slumber, he devoted himself to his task. A couple of hours passed without incident; but at last his vigilance was justified and rewarded. The ruffian at the rope who, while there remained a chance that any of his proposed victims might be still awake, had pulled with steady cadence the heavy punkahs, now began to simulate slumber, and at intervals to cease pulling. Evidently this was a deep and artful ruse to discover if the cessation of the fanning breeze might, peradventure, rouse any of the sleepers; but none of them stirred. The moment for action had clearly arrived. So the blood-thirsty coolie coughed a smothered cough once or twice as a signal to his two confederates in the verandah; but as no response came, he prepared to go and personally warn them. As a pecautionary measure, however, he noiselessly laid down the rope, and, approaching the nearest sleepers, bent over them to satisfy himself that they were really unconscious. As he repeated this performance over our watchful friend, whose hair was now standing on end with horror, he found himself suddenly clutched in the embrace of a pair of arms nerved with the strength of panic fear, while loud shouts of "I've got him! I've got him!" echoed through the room. Breathless with excitement, the bold captor told his thrilling tale, and demanded that the three villains should be led to instant execution. He laughed to scorn the plausible story of his captive, to the effect that he had been left at the punkah rope longer than his rightful turn, that he had coughed to attract the attention of his "budlee" or relieving coolie, that on this signal failing he had then determined to go and fetch him; but *dur ki maree*, "the fear of being beaten," had induced him to make sure, before doing so, that none of the "sahibs" was likely to jump up, and, *more Anglo-Indico*, chastise him. Fortunately for the wretched coolie his explanation was accepted, not without much laughter, and he escaped the gallows; but nothing could ever convince his gallant captor that he had not by his courage and presence of mind averted a dreadful massacre.

It is really difficult to exaggerate the demoralisation which at that period seemed to overcome the nerves of certain of the more weak-kneed among us. Every native was to their excited imagination a "Pandy." My own faithful bearer, Sheodeen, owed to the natty twist of his turban and the martial way in which he habitually curled up his moustaches, a very close interview with the hangman. He was, during my absence, arrested, and would undoubtedly have been given a short shrift if an officer who knew him had not sent for me in hot haste. My earnest advice to him after that grim experience was to roll his "puggrie" anyhow, to take the curl out of his moustaches, to drop his jaunty swaggering gait, and generally to look as mean and dirty as possible.

On the night of the 11th an adventure happened to myself, which at the time I was rather shy of mentioning, but which I may now relate. I had taken it on myself to do a little patrolling on my own account; and as I was starting from near the main gate of the "Dumdama," I came across a Eurasian Trumpeter named Murray, of my own regiment. As he was mounted I asked him to accompany me. This he did. We had not gone far before we saw, indistinctly, through the dusk, what appeared to be a small group of the rebels, cautiously creeping towards where a tree, growing close to the wall, gave them a fair chance of successfully scaling it. "Will you stick by me, Murray, and charge them?" I whispered. "That I will, sir," replied he: "I will stand by you to the last drop of my blood." So, drawing our swords, and moving quietly forward for a few yards, we suddenly clapped spurs to our horses and charged—to the bewilderment and complete demoralisation of a speckled cow, over whose body we narrowly escaped "coming to grief," and who, as soon as she could recover her senses, dashed off into the darkness. "Never mind, Murray," said I. "It might have been the Pandies, you know. We'll just say nothing about this—yet a while." Poor fellow! he was killed not many days afterwards, bravely fighting, at the Hindun Nuddee.

On the evening of the 15th May the native Sappers and Miners from Roorkee marched into Meerut. Next afternoon it so happened that a small party of the faithful remnant of the 3rd Light Cavalry, which was about to proceed under my command to the support of the civil authorities in a neighbouring station, was paraded, mounted, for the General's inspection, close to the barrack where he had taken up his quarters, when I heard the report of a single shot, rapidly followed by two or three more, from the direction of the Sapper Camp; and presently saw that a scene of confusion and uproar was going on there. A rumour reached me—how I do not remember—that the Sappers had mutinied, had killed Alfred Light, the artillery officer who afterwards became so distinguished, and were about to fly into the jungle. Naturally I lost no time in dismounting and running in to the barrack to inform

General Hewett, whom I found in the dishabille of shirt and pyjamas.

While I was making my report to the bewildered General, Brigadier Archdale Wilson pushed up to us, buckling on his sword-belt, and ordered me to mount at once and follow the Sappers and keep them in sight till he could come up with some of the Carabineers and guns. By this time the Sappers, who, I firmly believe, had at first no intention whatever of mutinying, but had been seized by sudden panic through groundless fear of an attack by the European troops, were swarming in flight over the plain, some in uniform, some in native clothes, but all armed with their muskets.

The shot which I had heard had been fired, as I subsequently learnt, by an Afghan, and had killed the Commanding Officer, Major Fraser. The action of this one man compromised all his comrades. However loyally disposed they might have been, they must have felt that now appearances were so fatally against them that no quarter could be hoped for from the enraged European troops who surrounded them; and that instant flight offered the only slender chance of escape from destruction.

As my little party galloped after them I was stopped by an artillery officer, evidently senior in rank to myself, who ordered me to halt and asked me where I was going. I told him that the Brigadier-General had ordered me to follow the Sappers who had mutinied and killed Alfred Light. "That is hardly possible," he said, "seeing that I am Alfred Light. These Sappers are not mutinying at all, but are going with permission to destroy a neighbouring village of budmashes. You stop where you are. I will take the responsibility." Taken quite aback by all this, I was still remonstrating with him when the Brigadier-General rode up, furious with me for having halted, and ordered me on again. I was glad to leave Alfred Light to settle the question of my delay with him, and dashed on in pursuit. Soon we overtook about fifty men, who took refuge in a grove of trees surrounded by a wall; and there I kept guard over them till the arrival of the Brigadier-General with a squadron of Carabineers and some guns. A few rounds were fired into the grove, but without much effect, and then dismounted Carabineers and a number of officers skirmished into it, and pursued the Sappers from tree to tree. The poor fellows fought with the energy of despair. No quarter was given, and all were destroyed, except two who were made prisoners by myself, and who, I believe, were afterwards retained in the service, and proved perfectly loyal.

At the close of this affair I noticed a man who had retreated through the grove and had taken refuge behind a low wall on its further side, from which shelter he betrayed himself by firing at us.

As I rode round the outside of the enclosure on its left and got in line with him, a Trooper of the Carabineers appeared at the opposite end of the wall, and we both came down on him at full gallop. The Sapper jumped to his feet and fixed his bayonet. We reached him almost at the same moment. As the Trooper lifted his sword to deliver a swinging cut the Sapper charged him with his bayonet and transfixed him through the breast, with a sickening ripping sound which still haunts my ears, while my straining sword arm failed by an inch to reach and lift the bayonet. Before he could withdraw the bayonet I had run him through the body. The uplifted arm of the Carabineer dropped, the sword slipped from his grasp, he reeled for a moment on his saddle, and then fell to the ground dead.

A correspondent wrote to the *Pioneer* :- "The Carabineer who was killed just outside Meerut in the Sapper Affair was a Trooper, named Frederick Kingsford, who rode an untrained horse, which became unsteady at the time of charging the rebel. He was the first man killed in action in the Mutiny, although many Europeans had fallen before that day."

It was late in the evening when we returned to cantonments. The destination of my small party, which was to have started next morning into the district, was unexpectedly changed.

A message had been received by General Hewett from a party of fugitives from Delhi, who were wandering about in the jungles near that place, and who implored that help should be sent to them. When I heard of this I felt that women and children could not possibly be left to their fate among the rebels without at least an effort being made to save them; so I went to General Hewett and offered to attempt the rescue with twenty-five men of the remnant of my regiment. He asked if I was in earnest, and told me that the fugitives had not got far from Delhi, and that he had considered it hopeless to send a succouring party. The letter, which was written in the French language, had been thrown under a table, whence I saw it picked up. The General then gave me permission, and on the forenoon of the 17th my party started. On our way out of Meerut we met Lieutenant Hugh Gough of our regiment (now Sir H. Gough, *V. C., K.C. B.*, commanding the Lahore Division). He told me that he had just heard of my having volunteered for this duty, and that he could not let me go alone. So he galloped back to get his arms, and thus, in this most gallant and self-sacrificing manner, came with me on an errand which both of us felt pretty sure was to be our last. We rode all day, expecting every moment our men to turn on us and bolt to Delhi. The temptation must have been very sore to them; for they had witnessed the extreme demoralisation which the Mutiny had caused in Meerut; but providentially they remained staunch. Only once did we meet with a show of opposition at a large village, but most fortunately we thought it probable that the inhabitants were alarmed at our French-grey uniforms, and took us for a party of mutineers on the prowl. So Gough and I halted the men and rode on alone. The sight of our white faces re-assured the villagers, and our explanations calmed them.

Late in the evening we arrived at the village of Hirchinpore, where we had ascertained from people in the fields that the fugitives were to be found. Again our light-grey uniforms caused alarm and confusion. The gate of a walled enclosure was shut in our faces, and it was with great difficulty that we got those inside to believe that we were friends. At last, on our promising to leave the men outside, Gough and I were admitted; and we rode in, not without suspicion that we might ourselves have fallen into a trap. We found a very dark old gentleman called Cohen, the zemindar of the village, an Orientalised Jew I think, seated in the doorway with a gun in his hand, evidently determined in case of treachery to sell his life dearly. The fugitives of whom we were in search had in despair stowed themselves away in various hiding places, and when they appeared presented a pitiable spectacle from the effects of the hardships they had undergone. All that night we had to remain there while Cohen's people collected carts to convey the women and children. If one of our men or one of the villagers had bolted and carried to Delhi the news of what a haul could be made at Hirchinpore, two or three hours would have sealed our fate. But again Providence befriended us, and early next morning our little caravan started for Meerut, where we safely arrived that night, and I had the joy of once more seeing my Sister, of whom I could not bear to take leave when I started, and who had been in ignorance of my having gone till I was miles on my way. The following are the names of the ladies and gentlemen who composed the party of fugitives:—

1. Colonel Knyvett, 38th Regiment, N. I.
2. Lieutenant Salkeld, Bengal Engineers. (Died of wounds received at the assault of Delhi).
3. Lieutenant Wilson, Bengal Artillery.
4. ,, Montague M. Proctor, 38th N. I.
5. ,, H. Gambier, 38th N. I. (Died of wounds received at the assault of Delhi).
6. Captain G. Forrest, *V. C.* (Died from the effects of injuries received in the defence of the Delhi Magazine on 11th May, 1857).
7. Lieutenant, Vibart, 54th N. I.
8. Mrs. Forrest,

9. Mrs. Fraser, widow of Major Fraser, who had been killed at Meerut by the mutineer sappers.
10. Miss Forrest.
11. ,, Annie Forrest.
12. ,, Eliza Forrest.
13. Mr. Marshall (merchant).
14 & 15. Two European women whose names I do not know.

Very glad was I to turn in that night with the prospect of a good rest, but I had not been asleep very long before the late Major Sanford, then a Lieutenant in my old regiment, and one of the most gallant gentlemen that ever buckled on a sword-belt, came and woke me up and told me that he had volunteered to carry despatches from General Hewett to the Commander-in-Chief at Umballa *viâ* Kurnal, and that he wanted me to escort him with my little faithful party. Of course I agreed, and went off to our lines, where the already tired men willingly consented to undertake the fresh and still more fatiguing and possibly more dangerous journey. Their horses were, however, quite knocked up, so I asked and obtained permission to select for them twenty-five of the partially-broken remounts of the Carabineers.

Early in the morning we paraded in the lightest of light marching order, the young horses vigorously resenting being so unceremoniously pressed into the ranks before passing through Riding School. For the first few miles there was not much order in our little column. The half-broken troopers rearing, buck-jumping and plunging about, had it pretty much their own way; but before night they were quiet enough. All day we marched, and all night, and all next day, halting for an hour or so at a time, when a wayside well enabled us to water the horses. We requisitioned feeds of grain for them and of chuppatis for ourselves as we went along, duly giving receipts for them. *En route* we made a long detour off the road to a district where we had been ordered to go in search of baggage-camels, which we were to have seized if we had found them; but they had departed. On the second day we met the late gallant Major (then Lieutenant) Hodson who, escorted by a party of the Jhind Horse, had started on his ride to Meerut with despatches from General Anson to General Hewett, and who was to return with despatches from the latter to Army Head-Quarters. So unexpected was this meeting that at first each party took the other for "moofsids," as we used in those days to designate the rebels; but we soon discovered our mistake. Hodson was naturally much relieved to find that the road in front of him was open, though doubtless disappointed that his errand was forestalled. The reader, who has read of Hodson's famous ride to Meerut, and who has not to this moment ever heard that it was anticipated by others, will probably be surprised by this narration, but nevertheless it is simply true. The credit of carrying the first despatches from Meerut to Umballa is due to the late Major Sanford, who, to me and to all who knew him, was a type of all that is most noble and brave and modest; but alas! his memory is buried in our hearts. The world has heard little of him.

In the evening we arrived at Kurnal, having traversed in less than thirty-six hours more than ninety miles: for the straight road between Meerut and Kurnal is seventy-six, and our fruitless detour after the camels took us many more miles. Sanford at once went on by dâk to Umballa and delivered his despatches to General Anson. He eventually got command of the cavalry of the guide corps before Delhi, and retained it till the close of the siege.

My small party was not then sent back to Meerut, but moved down towards Delhi with the advanced body of troops, making itself useful in collecting supplies and scouting. On the road we succeeded in capturing several miscreants who had committed murderous outrages on our unfortunate countrymen and women while trying to effect their escape from Delhi. They were given the benefit of a fair trial; and those who were found guilty were duly hanged.

One of these wretches who had been tried and sentenced one afternoon was subsequently confined till sunset—the usual hour for executions—in the guard tent of the 1st Bengal Fusiliers, which happened on that occasion to contain another tenant, an Irish soldier who had been drinking, "not wisely but too well." When the Provost Marshal's party came in the evening for the condemned criminal they found him in a sorry plight. The half-sober Irishman begged that they would not take him away. "Bedad," said he, "he has been the most divarting companion I iver had." The "divarsion" had been perhaps a little one-sided.

One evening, shortly before the force reached Alipore, I was suddenly ordered to take my party back to Meerut *viâ* Bagput, for the General expected an engagement, and evidently felt uncertain as to whether my men were to be trusted under such trying circumstances as an actual fight against their old comrades. Previously to this poor General Anson had died, worn out by anxiety and fatigue, and General Barnard was in command. Accompanied by the Adjutant-General, Colonel Chester, and by his Interpreter, Captain Howell, he inspected my little party on parade, and after praising its conduct in the highest terms, informed us that he would give each native member of it a step of substantive rank for each of the two expeditions in which they had shared. He then told them that in a short time he expected to engage the rebels, and that, though he had no doubt of their loyalty, he was unwilling to take them into action against men who so lately had been their comrades, of their own race and religions, and that therefore he had decided to send them back to Meerut. The whole of them implored to be allowed to remain and to prove their loyalty in the field; but the General was not to be turned from his decision. He was evidently much moved, and for a moment I hoped that he was wavering; but presently he turned away; and with deep disappointment I felt that there was nothing for it but to turn our horses' heads to the east and make for the ferry at Bagput. Before General Barnard could carry out his promise he fell a victim to cholera. Colonel Chester was killed in action, and Captain Howell also died—I think from that scourge of the camp—cholera. Thus was left on my shoulders the whole *onus* of securing to my men the fulfilment of the General's promise—a task in which, after much trouble and delay, I was happily eventually successful.

To march off the ground and out of camp no preparations were needed, for we were without camp equipage of any kind whatever. It must be remembered that all this took place in the middle of the hot weather, before the rains; so that it was no hardship to sleep in the open air on the ground beside our horses, who also required no blankets. Except our horses, their saddles and bridles and our arms, and the clothes on our backs, we possessed literally nothing in the world.

It was not long, therefore, before we had put a good distance between ourselves and our late comrades. When dawn broke we found ourselves debouching from a grove of trees on to a plain, at the further side of which was the river and the bridge-of-boats with the village of Bagput on the opposite bank; but to our horror the bridge was occupied by a strong body of apparently rebel troops, whom our appearance threw into sudden commotion. We could see infantry rapidly falling in, troopers mounting in hot haste, and camels and elephants rushing to the bridge, flying from our expected onslaught. Scant time was there to decide on a course of action. With our tired horses escape from so strong a body of cavalry was hopeless. Nothing was left but to charge the bridge and trust to luck and the rapidity of our attack to disconcert the enemy, and enable some at least of us to get through with whole skins. These were the days of drilling by "threes;" but as I judged that there would be room for four men abreast on the bridge, I formed my party as quickly as possible into what would now be called a column of sections of fours, and moved down the slope on to the plain at a gallop, increasing our pace as we approached the bridge. To my delight and surprise the enemy seemed quite demoralised and in confusion, and I was beginning to feel sure of a successful rush through them, when I was startled by the apparition of a white face peering at me from behind a mass of stones, and the shout of an English voice yelling at me to halt. Never was man more relieved and pleased to be out of a frightful scrape. In another second I had halted my party and had ridden across the bridge and was talking to——, an officer who informed me that he had been sent with a strong body of the Raja of Jhind's troops to occupy the bridge and hold it till further orders; but he said that he was not going to stay any longer. The place was a great deal too near Delhi and too liable to sudden attack to please him, and the fright he had got from the sudden appearance of my small party had put the finishing touch to his resolution. He said that our French-grey uniforms and the swiftness of our attack had convinced him that we were the advanced party of a large body of the enemy, and he had given himself up for lost. At any rate he had had enough of Bagput and meant to be off at once. In vain I implored him to defer his departure till the evening, pointing out that my horses were quite done up, and that we would be obliged to stop there for some hours to rest and feed. Nothing would move him, and there and then he marched off, bag and baggage, and left us to our own devices. We could plainly hear the guns of a fight, which must have been that at the Hindun Nuddee; and, tired as we were, rest was impossible. In the afternoon we moved on, and next morning marched into Meerut without further misadventure.

III.

BEFORE DELHI.

FOR the next few weeks time passed quietly enough with me. The greater portion of the garrison of Meerut had gone to strengthen the besieging force at Delhi; and had, under Brigadier-General Archdale Wilson, at the hard fought battles at the Hindun Nuddee, gloriously wiped away the reproach of the supine inaction which had been imposed on it by General Hewett on the 10th of May. We, who were left to kick our heels in idleness at Meerut, spent most of our time in moving Heaven and Earth to get transferred to the army at Delhi. At last the red-letter-day came for me. My friend and comrade, Captain Sanford, had been appointed to officiate in the command of the Cavalry of the Guides Corps, and he lost no time in writing to me and promising that if

I could get over to Delhi, he would manage to have me attached to the regiment. At that moment I was laid up with a touch of fever, due probably to previous exposure; but I was not long in presenting myself to the Staff Officer of the garrison and shewing him Sanford's letter, taking very good care not to remind him that I was on the sick list—a circumstance which he fortunately overlooked. That afternoon I joyfully took French leave of the Doctor, and started in company with some half-dozen other officers, who were also bound for the Delhi force, back again along the well-remembered track to Bagput. We marched at night, thinking that we were then, more likely than in the day time, to escape encounter with any prowling bands of rebels or Goojars. The district between Meerut and Bagput was infested by the latter, a tribe of hereditary criminals whose chief amusement during peaceful times seems to consist in effecting breaches of the Penal Code, while they invariably take advantage of periods of disturbance to indulge to the utmost their ingrained predatory propensities. Small as our party was, we were therefore careful to adopt all practical precautions. As I knew the road I was sent in advance as a scout, while on each flank rode another officer, the main body of three or four men detaching one more to the rear. In this order we rode all night, fortunately without adventure; and in the gray dawn we reached Bagput.

The bridge-of-boats had been removed, and we crossed the river in a large flat-bottomed ferry boat. Here we had the misfortune to lose one of our horses, belonging to Captain Craigie of my regiment. His owner had neglected to unfasten the rather tight standing-martingale which he always used; and this hampered the animal when it tried to jump into the boat, and caused it to fall into the deep water between it and the bank. Even now all would have been well but for that unlucky standing-martingale which entirely prevented the struggling horse from swimming, and held its nose hopelessly under water till it was drowned, without any possibility of help being given it. In a few moments the poor horse sank, carrying with it Craigie's saddle and bridle and a revolver which was in one of the holsters. The efforts which some native divers made to recover the saddle, &c., were fruitless; and we had to abandon the endeavour, borrow a "country" nag for Craigie, and cross the river. When we reached the opposite bank we heard shouts from the Bagput side, and saw men holding up the saddle and revolver which they had succeeded in fishing up. That was, however, the last that Craigie saw of his property. As we crossed the stretch of sand on the further bank we narrowly escaped another casualty; for one of our party got into a quicksand, and for some moments horse and man were in serious danger of being swallowed up. At last, however, we all got safely under way and continued the second half of our journey.

Never shall I forget the moment when, from a rising ground, the frowning walls of Delhi and the white tents of the besieging force burst into view.

So vast an extent of ground was covered by the huge city—so puny and diminutive in comparison was the encampment which nestled under the famous "Ridge!" Truly a sight to fill the heart with exulting pride; for we knew that the men in these tent were sure, some day before many weeks were over, to storm the formidable walls of the great fortress, and to carry the British flag in triumph into its innermost citadel. No shadow of doubt of the ultimate success of our arms ever troubled any of our minds in those days. The insolent belief in the irresistibility of the *furor Britannicus* had not then met any of the rude shocks which in latter days have somewhat shaken it, in spite of an army composed of short-service soldiers and of leaders trained to a pitch of theoretical perfection by the Professors of the Staff College.

Directly we arrived in camp I reported myself to Sir Henry Norman, then Assistant Adjutant-General of the Force, and, I think, in rank a captain. In a few hours I was put in orders as attached to the Cavalry of the Guides. The famous forced march of that splendid corps under Daly from Hoti Murdan to Delhi is matter of history, and can never be forgotten. The honourable roll of its losses in officers and men during the siege is recorded on a tablet on the wall of the memorial tower on the Ridge.

I do not propose to inflict on the reader's patience the often-told story of the siege. That task has been performed by far abler pens than mine. It will be sufficient for me to endeavour to sketch two or three of the minor episodes at which I was present, and which seemed to me to be picturesque or interesting.

As may be easily understood, much of our time in the Cavalry branch was occupied on picquet or outpost duty. One of these outposts, at a place called, I think, Azadpore, far away on the extreme right rear of our position, was peculiarly liable to attack, as it was pretty well "in the air," and offered a tempting object for a sudden swoop by a large body of the enemy. One afternoon when my commanding officer, Captain Sanford, and myself, being off duty, were mounting to enjoy a quiet ride, we became aware of a great commotion in the Azadpore direction. Clouds of dust rapidly whirling in the air! Camels and grass-cutters' ponies flying wildly to the camp! Evidently something wrong! "Gallop to the lines. Sound the Boot-and-Saddle and the Mount" was the order Captain Sanford gave me, while he tore off into the clouds of dust to reconnoitre. Instantly was the quiet of our camp changed into a scene of the liveliest bustle. Horses being saddled—men tumbling out of their tents—buckling on their belts—jumping on their horses, and "falling in"—all this in frantic haste—when Sanford returned and shouted to me "Bring along as many men as have mounted. Never mind telling off. The Azadpore picquet is being driven in." By this time not more than 20 or 25 men were in their saddles, and away we went after Sanford as hard as we could tear, leaving the rest of the regiment to follow as soon as it could be got together. Through the flying animals and camp followers, many of them wounded, we galloped along, straining our eyes into the distance; and presently we saw the picquet, surrounded by clouds of the rebel horse, being driven slowly back, stubbornly fighting and disputing every inch of ground. As we hove into sight the enemy more or less disengaged itself from the picquet, and attempted to throw itself into formation to meet our attack. There must have been several hundred of them. The whole ground in front seemed thick with them; and I must confess my heart sank within me when the gallant Sanford, instead of waiting for the reinforcements which must have been close behind us, simply increased the pace, and evidently meant to hurl our small party straight into the overwhelming mass before us. "It is all up with you this time" was my ejaculation to myself, but "needs must" when —one's commanding officer leads! So I set my teeth and determined to make the best of a bad job. Could I believe my eyes? The dense body that had begun to advance against us slowed down to a walk—halted—wavered—and finally scattered! With a roar we charged into them. Our pace was so great that it was impossible for them to put on the steam in time to escape our onslaught. The picquet joined in—our own reinforcements caught us up—and then was seen on that plain as pretty a bout of sword play as ever rejoiced the heart of a horseman. No attempt at keeping order was possible. As the "Pandies" scattered, so did we, each man singling out his victim. The slaughter of the enemy was considerable, the losses on our side extremely trifling. As the fierce pursuit rolled on we became aware that the masses of the flying mutineers were thickening in our front, and were gradually concentrating towards one point. Evidently some obstruction prevented their escape to the flanks. At last a huge living wedge of frantic, struggling, panic-stricken men and horses was crowded together, hemmed in between a deep canal and a masonry aqueduct which crossed it at right angles. Into this solid mass it was impossible to penetrate, but the outer fringe of it was mowed down by the *tulwars* of our men. No quarter was ever given or taken before Delhi. If the mutineers had been cruel as the most savage of wild beasts, fearful was the revenge which many and many a time was wreaked on them by our maddened troops.

Where the aqueduct crossed the canal it had been partially destroyed, and on the masses of fallen masonry it was just possible for one horseman at a time to pick his way across; but where one escaped many were overthrown and trampled on by the struggling mob

It had been comparatively easy for the enemy, intent on the surprise of the Azadpore picquet, to steal across in single file; but it was quite a different thing for a confused and terrified crowd to force its way across. At this point great slaughter took place, and many, in despair, turned round and charged their pursers, only to meet a certain and speedy death. One poor wretch, extricating himself from the crowd, jumped his horse on to a detached fragment of the broken aqueduct on the plain before it joined the canal, and there he stood, as on a pedestal six or eight feet high, in vain seeking a short respite from his inevitable fate. Almost simultaneously one of our men sprung his horse alongside of him, and on that precarious platform, with barely footing for their horses, these two engaged in a savage fight for life. Like lightning their swords flashed as they cut at each other without any attempt at parrying. In a second or two our man received a frightful slash on his arm, and it would have gone hard with him if at that moment one of his comrades who was armed with a long spear had not charged straight at the group, and, as he pulled his horse up on its haunches at the base of the masonry, transfixed the Pandy through the body. At the same instant our man, maddened with pain and excitement, drove his horse against his antagonist and thrust him clean off the block of masonry, horses and men all rolling together on the ground below.

The survivors of the adventurous spirits who had attacked the outpost rode back into Delhi that night considerably crestfallen.

The picquet had been furnished by one of the Punjab cavalry regiments, and was commanded by a gentleman of a rather taciturn habit who is still well remembered under his nickname of "Fowls." Never shall I forget the quaint but gallant spectacle which he presented, as with his faithful quizzing glass firmly glued on to one eye he faced his enemies and laid about him with his sword, grimly silent, while being slowly driven back by the *force majeure* of overwhelming numbers. The story goes that he earned his *petit nom* as follows:—On some occasion, on the line of march, he had, for days and weeks, ridden solemnly and silently among his comrades. Not a word had ever escaped his lips till, on one memorable morning, as his detachment entered a village, our friend, who must have been gloomily pondering on the scantiness of the supplies in the camp larder of the mess, espied a family of *moorgis* busily scratching up the dust on the road before him. The welcome sight was too much for him. Then and there he lifted up his voice and cried "Fowls!" and straightway relapsed into pristine dumbness. Seldom if ever has so short a speech been greeted with such loud applause. His delighted comrades, now that the spell was broken, naturally hoped that the sudden ejaculation was but a preliminary to a permanent loosening of the hitherto tied tongue; but they were doomed to disappointment. From that time forth not a word escaped those lips. Neither fowls nor ducks nor geese nor turkeys, nor even sheep availed any more to draw forth the slightest oral token of appreciation—merely would the half sleepy eyes glisten into life at the sight of the welcome "find," and possibly a nod of the head would direct attention to it. Thus came it about that the soubriquet of "Fowls" was by unanimous vote conferred on its possessor.

That evening when we were all assembled at dinner in the mess tent, an unfortunate "Pandy" who had been found skulking under a bush by some of our men was brought before the commanding officer. There was no mistaking him for anything but a sepoy; and there could be no doubt about his fate. Still I could not help thinking his luck was very hard; and doubtless my face betrayed my feelings; for the unfortunate man, with an appealing look at me, declared he was no sepoy, but had been my domestic servant; and he implored me to bear witness to his truth and save his life. What could I do! It was impossible to swear to a falsehood; but I pleaded hard, though, I fear, unsuccessfully, that he might be allowed to escape.

During one of the numerous encounters with the enemy which kept the camp before Delhi lively, an officer serving with the infantry of the Guides Corps was wounded in a manner sufficiently curious to deserve record. During a pause in the operations he was standing with his back to a tree when a bullet struck the ground close to him, and caused a fragment of stone to fly up against his forehead, on which it inflicted a slight flesh wound. As he threw his head back at the sudden shock, it came in contact with a sharp splinter of a broken branch sticking out from the tree. Instinctively he put his right hand up to his forehead. It was covered with blood. Then he felt the back of his head with his left hand. That also was all bloody. "My God!" He exclaimed, "I'm a dead man! Shot right through the head!" and he sought a soft place to lie down on and die, an event which he expected to take place in a second or two. To his surprise, after fully a minute, he was as alive as ever. . So, again, he felt the two wounds. There was no mistake about it. They were both bleeding freely. Once more he curled himself up; but as death did not come, he presently began to think that there must be something strange and abnormal about the hole right through his head, and his relief may be imagined, when a brother officer, after a hurried examination of it, explained matters to him. I am afraid he was flippant enough, as he jumped to his feet, to join in the laugh against himself. Wonderful recoveries from apparently mortal wounds were by no means uncommon. I have myself seen an officer hit full in the chest by a bullet which came out at his back. I jumped off my horse and wrung his hand for the last farewell, and rode on (for this occurred during a pursuit), leaving him to the care of the surgeon who at that moment came up. What was my surprise to find, many hours afterwards when we returned to camp, that the wounded officer was not only not dead, but not likely to die. The bullet had glanced off a rib and gone round his chest under the skin, and so out of his back. Another officer had his jaw smashed by a bullet which did not apparently make its exit anywhere. The simple fact was that he swallowed it, along with some of his teeth.

On the Ridge stood a lofty building, the Observatory Tower, from the summit of which, during the early part of the siege, a look-out used to be kept on the operations of the enemy.

This fact becoming known, drew on the tower an altogether undesirable share of attention from the guns on the walls of Delhi; and the upper parts of it soon got considerably knocked about by shot and shell. Long after this look-out post had been withdrawn occasional shells used still to be "loosed off" at the tower, making things rather hot for the small knot of officers off duty which used generally to be found up there enjoying the view when anything more interesting than usual was going on in front. On one occasion two or three other men and myself had found our way to the top of it, when we were joined by a gentleman connected with a mercantile firm, to whose enterprise the camp was indebted for its supplies of "tar bund" beer (a luxury for which we were glad to pay sixteen rupees a dozen), Exshaw's brandy and Harvey's sauce, and many varieties of tinned provisions, besides Holloway's pills and ointment, and such like patent nostrums. While we were all looking at the walls of the city, a puff of white smoke was seen to issue from a point known to us as "the hole in the wall" where dwelt a mortar of large calibre. In a few seconds the big shell vomited out from it burst high in the air, fully a quarter of a mile away from us, but in a very accurate alignment for our position. "Down," shouted one of our number, and we all, with the exception of our civilian friend, crouched behind a heavy mass of solid masonry. He, however, stood his ground, folded his arms across his chest, and for a moment surveyed us with a look of half contemptuous surprise. "Why have these stupid fellows sought shelter?" thought he. "The shell has burst ever so far away. The danger is all over now. The pieces must be falling to the ground." Very speedily was he undeceived. Hurtling and hissing, the broken fragments of the shell came rushing onwards and crashed against the tower, fortunately without hitting him. As we stood up he threw himself down. He then learned a lesson, which I dare say he did not soon forget, concerning the momentum of projectiles, and the general advisability of taking a hint from persons presumably likely to know what they were about.

All this time the siege, if so it could be described, "dragged its slow length along;" but in reality, neither was the

City invested by us, nor was our force besieged, as has been so often asserted, by the rebel troops. Both forces lay facing each other. Both were in contact along a comparatively short front. Both were entirely open to their respective rear, with practically unmenaced communications in those directions. Neither could prevent reinforcements or supplies reaching the other. We on our part could not even attempt to intercept the various contingents of mutineers which, during the early part of the siege, poured into Delhi from the south; and were hurled, in almost monotonous succession, against our position, while still fresh and undemoralised by defeat, only to be driven back, time after time, with immense slaughter, by the invincible little phalanx of Britons, Sikhs and Gurkhas, which sturdily clung, bull-dog fashion, to the ground it had taken up. For a time the numbers of the enemy continued to increase, as almost daily fresh bodies by regiments and brigades marched into the already crowded city, their arrival noisily saluted by heavy artillery. Our muster roll, on the other hand, far from augmenting, actually dwindled away; for incessant losses from casualties in action were heavily supplemented by deaths from fever and cholera; and our much-needed reinforcements were long in coming. But we rested secure in the firm assurance that sooner or later they would certainly come. We all knew that John Lawrence and his lieutenants were straining every nerve to secure the safety of the Punjab in our rear, by disarming the disaffected Hindustani regiments in that province, and by raising fresh ones, both of cavalry and infantry, from the staunch fighting men of the Khalsa. We knew that as swiftly as could possibly be compassed by human forethought and human energy, these trustworthy and brave levies, and every British regiment that could be spared, and every heavy gun and mortar in the Ferozepore Arsenal, and, almost better than all, the heroic Nicholson would come to our aid; and that then the real siege would begin in earnest, and the fate of Delhi would be sealed.

Early in August took place the only serious effort on the part of the enemy to cut off our communications. To quote from a letter written by General Wilson to Nicholson and received by the latter on the 3rd of August*:—"The enemy have re-established the bridge over the Najufgurh Canal (which we had destroyed) and have established themselves in force there, with the intention of moving on Alipore and our communications with the rear. I therefore earnestly beg you to push forward with the utmost expedition in your power, both to drive these fellows from my rear, and to aid me in holding my position." How promptly and effectually Nicholson carried out these instructions is graphically described in the pages of Sir John Kaye's work. On the 14th of August he led into the Delhi Camp the moveable

---

* *Kaye's Sepoy War*, Vol. II, p. 645.

column which had already done yeoman's service by disarming the mutinous regiments at Phillour and Umritsar, and destroying the Sealkote Brigade of rebels at Trimmoo Ghât. On the 25th of August he marched out again at the head of a small force of all arms; and before nightfall he had swept from Najufgurh the "Neemuch Brigade" which was lying in wait to intercept the siege train on its slow approach from Ferozepore Arsenal.

There are some men whose personal appearance harmonises so perfectly with their intellectual and moral characteristics that any one on seeing them for the first time would be almost certain intuitively to guess their identity. Nicholson was one of these. Tall, dark, and stern, he looked every inch what he was, a fearless, self-reliant, fierce and masterful man, born for stormy times and stirring events. It was impossible to associate him with anything commonplace, or otherwise than heroic or great. On me, as on every one else, he produced a vivid impression, which can never become dim. When I first saw him it was only for a moment. He said something in low tones to an acquaintance, and passed on ; but instinctively I felt that I had come into contact with one who stood apart from and overtopped other men. "That is Nicholson" I said, knowing that it could be no one else.

On the 4th of September the huge guns and mortars of the siege train, fitly drawn by still more colossal elephants, slowly and solemnly rolled through the camp on to the Ridge. On the 6th the very last batch of reinforcements, a detachment of the 60th Rifles from Meerut, arrived, marching " in their usual jaunty way" as described by Hervey Greathead in a letter to his wife written on that day. The Royal Engineers had already filled a vast " Engineers' park " with fascines, gabions, sand bags, and every conceivable appliance for the bombardment and storm. Nothing had been overlooked. Nothing remained but to begin the real and final siege and deliver the assault.

That no time was lost is evidenced by the fact that one breaching battery of six heavy guns, within seven hundred yards of the Moree Bastion, was finished and armed on the evening of the 6th, and began its work of destruction on the 7th.

IV.

STORMING THE CITY.

FROM that time till the morning of the 11th, when the last of the four batteries was completed, our gallant Engineers and working parties and Gunners worked as men have never worked before or since. All night long picks and spades and shovels were busily plied, under a heavy fire, in constructing the batteries; on which, so soon as finished, the heavy guns and mortars were mounted; and as successively they were placed in position they joined in swelling the furious storm of shot and shell which never ceased tearing down the masonry of the city defences till the moment of the assault in the grey dawn of the 14th. The last battery was built under the shelter of the ruined walls of the Custom-house, at a distance of 180 yards from the water bastion, under a terrific and incessant fire from the Kashmir and Water bastions and the curtain between them. Let the reader try to realise this; and he will admit that no more desperate or daring enterprise was ever achieved in front of a besieged fortress.

On the 13th it was my hard fate to be on outpost duty at Azadpore, where rumours reached me that the assault was likely to be delivered before dawn on the 14th. My picquet should in ordinary course have been relieved that morning, but no relief came; and as the day wore on, it seemed that I was destined to be left out there kicking my heels, forlorn and forgotten, till all should be over. This was more than could be borne; so I despatched messenger after messenger into camp with imploring letters, begging for the recall of my picquet. My entreaties were successful, and I had the intense, if selfish, gratification of at length seeing in the distance the small column of dust which heralded the approach of the party that had been sent to take my place. Very grumpy and sulky was the officer in command; but, after all, it was his turn for the duty. Every one must take his luck as it comes. Consoling him with this crusted old apothegm, I lost no time in clearing out of the post and taking my detachment back to camp; but even then I was destined to grievous disappointment. The troops intended to form the Cavalry Brigade under Sir Hope Grant had been told off, and my party had to content itself with forming part of the reserve which remained in camp. So I lost the chance of being one of the glorious six hundred, whose heroic endurance that day under a fierce hurricane of grape and musketry "prevented the enemy, who had driven back the 4th Column, from advancing along the open ground between the Ridge and the City, and taking the whole of our left attack in flank."* When the attempt of the column under the gallant Colonel Reid to force an entrance into the City by the Lahore Gate failed, partly owing to the want of artillery, and partly to

* *Kaye's Sepoy War.*

the defeat of the auxiliary Kashmir contingent, the whole brunt of keeping the victorious rebels, many thousands in numbers, from pouring out of Kissengunge and pursuing our retreating infantry, fell on the Cavalry Brigade. Before, however, the enemy could dare to trust themselves on the plain beyond the shelter of their walls, it was necessary to drive the horsemen from it; and fierce was the effort to do so. From the walls of the City, from the suburbs of Kissengunge, a fiery hail of lead unceasingly swept. Saddle after saddle was emptied; horse after horse fell, but not for a moment was there the slightest wavering or unsteadiness. Quietly and without confusion the ranks continued to close together and fill ever-recurring gaps, grimly determined to hold their ground to the last man. Utterly unable to return the fire, or to do anything but remain immoveable as passive living targets, they seemed doomed to eventual annihilation—when Tomb's famous troop of horse artillery galloped to the rescue. Taking up a position at the closest of close quarters, not more than two hundred yards from the enemy, it was not long after our guns came into action that they drove the hitherto trumphant rebels back from the external walls into the labyrinth of houses in their rear, and materially reduced their fire. But from the Lahore Gate an unsilenced 24-pounder still continued to pour grape into the ranks, and to tear many a ghastly gap in them. Not till the rebel fire, drawn off by the success of our attack on the Kashmiri Gate, had dwindled away to harmlessness, and all danger of a sortie was effectually extinguished, was the sorely crippled Cavalry Brigade withdrawn from its post of honour.

Though this deed of the six hundred before the walls of Delhi has not been sung by the Poet Laureate, and is not so world-famous as that of the other six hundred at Balaclava, it fully deserves to be bracketed with it as an example of heroism and self-sacrificing devotion. Each is a brilliant instance of the perfect union of discipline and courage. If the charge of the Light Brigade was a blunder, so much the greater is the glory of the brave men who rode to death without questioning their orders.

> Theirs not to reason why,
> Theirs but to do and die.

There was no blunder in the order which devoted the six hundred of the Delhi Cavalry to face a *feu d'enfer* for the salvation of their Infantry comrades. Every soldier who knows what it is to "sit still to be shot at" will appreciate with pride the feat of arms performed on that morning of the 14th September 1857 by the British and Native Cavalry Brigade under the command of the fearless and gentle Sir Hope Grant.

So vivid is the description of this episode in the glowing pages of Sir John Kaye that I find it difficult to resist the temptation of transcribing it; but most of my military readers are doubtless familiar with it; and if any have not yet read his *History of the Sepoy War in India*, I would recommend them to lose

THE KASHMIR GATE, DELHI.

no time in studying that deeply interesting work. It is an imperishable tribute to the glory of our arms, and no one who reads its narrative of the brave deeds done by Englishmen, civilians as well as soldiers, aided by Sikhs and Gurkhas and the few other loyal races of India during that time of supreme stress and trial, can help feeling his heart fill with honest and patriotic pride, and with confident hope that if ever again so fierce a struggle should be forced on ourselves or our descendants, the old spirit of the Anglo-Saxon race will prove true to itself.

I will not attempt to describe the various fortunes of the four columns of assault. That story has been told once for all by Sir John Kaye; and it is not likely that any more full or clear or correct narrative will ever be written.

Full of triumph as we who remained outside were at the knowledge that the Kashmiri Gate and curtain had been successfully stormed, and that our flag was flying on the ramparts which had so long defied us, it was yet inexpressibly mournful to witness the long procession of "doolies" bearing the dead and wounded which streamed slowly back into camp. Many a gallant soldier that day gave his life for the honour of his Queen and country; but the loss that overshadowed all others was that of the valiant Nicholson, struck down with a mortal wound in the hour of victory while nobly exposing himself to almost certain death in the act of cheering forward his men, who were for a moment checked by a torrent of lead that swept the narrow lane up which they were advancing. His memory and his example will never be lost to the British Army, long and brilliant as is the roll of its heroes.

The strength of the four columns of assault was 3,660 men ; of the Reserve column 1,500; or a total of 5,160. Opposed to us was a fortress " seven miles in circumference, filled with an immense fanatical Mussalman population, garrisoned by full 40,000 soldiers armed and disciplined by ourselves, with 114 heavy pieces of artillery mounted on the walls, with the largest magazine of shot, shell, and ammunition in the Upper Provinces at their disposal, besides some 60 pieces of field artillery, all of our own manufacture, and manned by artillerymen drilled and taught by ourselves."*

The casualties on our side that morning were 1,145 killed and wounded. The result of the day's fighting was that we had forced our way into a small corner of the City, and there "hung on by our teeth." Slight and precarious as was the grip which we had thus obtained on the throat of the enemy, it yet proved sufficient for eventual success; but there can be no dispute that for the next forty-eight hours the position was critical. The great City with its intricate network of narrow lanes crookedly piercing through masses of lofty brick-built houses —with its strong places such as the Magazine, the King's Palace, Selimgurh, and

---

* Colonel Wilson's letter to Colonel Baird Smith, dated 30th August, 1857.

the Jumma Musjid—was yet unconquered and defiant; the roar of combat continued without ceasing. The General, Sir Archdale Wilson, worn out with illness and want of rest, and with the strain of long-continued anxiety, seemed to those around him to be losing heart and to be half inclined to abandon our dearly-earned footing within the walls, and to withdraw the troops once more to the old position outside. Worse than all, great stores of brandy and wine which had been cunningly left by the rebels exposed to the sight of our soldiers, fell into their hands, and the inevitable result followed. Numbers of our men eagerly swallowed the fiery poison; and those who had hitherto proved themselves heroes now wallowed in the gutters, helpless and imbecile. Most providentially the enemy did not seize upon that moment for a vigorous onslaught. If they had done so it would probably have been successful, and the British Empire in India would have staggered under a crushing and shameful blow from the worst and most persistent foe of its army, strong drink. Vigorous measures were, however, promptly taken. Working parties, strongly officered, were told off to destroy the bottles and empty the casks; and very soon all danger from this source was averted.

On the 16th an important step in advance was achieved. The magazine was taken with trifling loss; and though the small arms portion of it had suffered seriously from the gallant exploit of Willoughby, who had blown it up on the 11th of May, great stores of artillery munitions were found in it. Very promptly were mortars set in position within it to shell the Palace, which was not more than a quarter of a mile distant. Most interesting and beautiful was it to see the big shells, propelled by a mere spoonful of powder, issuing from their wide throats; and, after performing a slow and graceful curve, easily followed by the naked eye, fall within the dull red walls of the Palace. Then would be heard a deep roar and a crash as of falling masonry, often followed by loud yells of hurt or dismay.

The next important forward move was accomplished on the night of the 18th and early morning of the 19th, when our troops, steadily working their way from house to house and enclosure to enclosure, succeeded in seizing the Lahore bastion. From this moment the game was all up for the enemy. The old King and his people had cleared out of the Palace on the 18th, doubtless finding the place inconveniently lively, and on the 19th a general exodus from the City must have been accomplished.

Early on the morning of the 20th my Commanding Officer, Captain Sanford, was nowhere to be found. I was told that he had last been seen riding, followed by a single orderly, in the direction of the City. In a moment flashed on me, with the confidence of certainty, the thought that he must have gone on a scouting expedition into the City, to ascertain how far the enemy had evacuated it, and that he had not taken me, usually his inseparable companion, because he did not wish to expose me to the risks of a certainly hare-brained exploit. No sooner had I formed this idea than I summoned my personal orderly and went off in search of him. When we arrived at the City my surmise was confirmed. Sanford and his orderly had been seen riding in to the deserted streets beyond our sentries. So we followed his example, and, keeping an uncommonly bright look-out, started on the route which he was said to have taken. Truly the town was abandoned. Not a living creature did we see; but we had not gone many hundred yards before we met Sanford, briskly trotting back, his face radiant with joy. He had penetrated right through the City to the Delhi and Turkman gates on the south, and had chalked "Guide Cavalry" on them. With him I rode to the quarters of Sir Archdale Wilson, to whom he reported the fact that the whole place was evacuated by the enemy. Whether others had anticipated Sanford I know not; but I do not think that whatever news may have been brought in to our Intelligence Department by native spies, any Englishman had, before him, with his own eyes, witnessed the fact that Delhi was at last entirely in our power. At any rate his daring exploit was performed exactly as I have related it. Not many months subsequently he lost his life, as will be hereafter told, while undertaking, single-handed, a not dissimilar reconnaisance.

During the day our troops entered into full possession of the City. All the strong points, the Palace, Selimgurh, the Jumma Musjid, the bastions and the gates were occupied by them; and the latest, and, let us trust, the last, siege of Delhi came to an end.

All is well that ends well. It is always easy and not always unprofitable after an event to speculate as to what might have been the result if a different course of action had been adopted with the view of bringing it about. It is well known that General Barnard, yielding to the arguments of the ardent young offi-

THE JUMMA MUSJID, DELHI.

cers of Royal Engineers, Greathead, Chesney, and Maunsell, aided by Hodson, had sanctioned an attempt to take Delhi by a *coup de main* on the morning of the 12th of June; and that if Brigadier Graves, the field officer of the day, had understood, or, understanding, had obeyed his instructions to reinforce the attacking column with the 1st Fusiliers, the assault would actually have come off. It is also known that about three weeks afterwards the General had again all but made up his mind to risk "the gambler's throw," when he first hesitated, and then decided to delay a little longer; that then he died of cholera; and that General Reed, who succeeded him, was compelled by broken health, after a few days, to resign the command into the hands of General Archdale Wilson; and that the latter never for a moment dreamed of doing more than holding his own position, far less of storming Delhi, till he had been reinforced by every available soldier that could be sent to him from the Punjab, and by the heavy guns and mortars of the siege train from Ferozepore.

It is certainly possible that if the intended assault had been delivered on the 12th of June it would have been successful. For my own part I have very little doubt on the subject. The battles of the Hindun Nuddee and of Badle-ka-Serai had severely shaken the *morale* of the enemy; and the very audacity of so daring and so prompt an attack by the united forces from Umballa and Meerut, each of which had, unsupported by the other, won so signal a victory, would have struck terror into the rebels and probably insured their defeat. On the other hand, the prospects of success three weeks later were not so hopeful. In the interval our numbers had not augmented, while those of the enemy had received considerable accessions. They had materially strengthened their defences; and had probably regained confidence in themselves.

Granting, however, that we would have succeeded in storming the walls, and even—far harder task—in driving the enemy out of the City with our handful of troops, would our position then have been better and stronger than the one we held on the Ridge? Would our two thousand bayonets have been adequate to occupy a circle of walls seven miles in length against an army of at least forty thousand men? For it may be presumed that as brigade after brigade and contingent after contingent mutinied they would have rolled together and attempted the recapture of the seat of the Moghul Empire. On the other hand, would the early fall of Delhi have prevented the further spread of revolt, and, if so, would that have been an unmixed good; or was it better that the full measure of the latent disaffection should be allowed to reveal itself and be once for all effectually stamped out? Such are the problems which will occur to a thoughtful mind and which cannot with certainty be solved.

The story of the capture of the old King and of the slaughter of the Princes by Hodson is too well-known to need repetition.

During the next few weeks nothing more eventful occurred within the walls of Delhi than the doings of the prize agents—from the point of view, at any rate, of a needy subaltern who looked to them for the replenishment of a purse which had been well nigh emptied by the incendiary fires at Meerut.

The first column to be detached on external operations was the one under Colonel Greathead of the 8th King's, which moved southwards with the view of attacking and breaking up any retreating bodies of the enemy which it might overtake; and which, early in October, so opportunely effected the relief of Agra, and gained so glorious a victory over the Indore contingent and the other rebel troops which were moving to the assault of that place. Another column under Brigadier-General Showers was subsequently sent into the districts to the west and north-west, and to this the Guide Cavalry was attached. Our chief object was to punish, and, if possible, capture the Nawab of Jhujjur; but before effecting this we moved about the country, "showing our muscle," to use a slang phrase, and thereby dispersing stray bands of marauders, and instilling confidence into the quietly disposed people of the agricultural classes.

During the suppression of the Mutiny, a campaign which was unique and unlike any other, the iron bands of discipline were, in some respects, not so tightly drawn as usual, and many things happened which would now be impossible. For instance, it was not at all unheard of for an enterprising officer, with no other sanction than that of his commanding officer, to take a small party of mounted men and start off on the prowl in search of adventures. Very frequently he found them, and took good care, in view of the irregularity of his proceedings, that no report of them reached the General. On some such occasion, a captain who was doing duty with us, and who was well-known for his eccentricity, almost verging on insanity, his fearlessness, and his unsparing thirst for vengeance against the mutineers, found himself, with a squad of sixteen or twenty men, many miles from camp, in front of the gateway of a walled enclosure, inside which were about forty rebel sepoys who, relying on their distance from danger, had taken no precautions against surprise, and were quietly cooking their dinner. H——took in the situation at once. "Halt!" he shouted in a stentorian voice, to his men, adding in Hindustani "Only twenty men follow me into the gate. Let the rest of the regiment remain outside." "Throw down your arms in that corner," he roared to the terror-stricken sepoys. "Gather together in the opposite corner, and be quick about it, or I will slay you all." He was immediately obeyed. "Now," said he, "I see among you a number of men older than the others, whom they have probably led astray. Drive them out from among you, that I may destroy them." The miserable cowards of young men instantly thrust out the older ones, struggling and fighting for dear life: and H——and his party fell on them and killed them.

Then turning to the traitorous remnant, "What dirt have you eaten! Oh children of owls!" and he "smote them also, hip and thigh."

Before utterly and unreservedly condemning this undoubtedly savage action, I would beg the reader to remember that in this Mutiny war no quarter was given on either side. We looked, and rightly looked, upon the mutineers, not as honest enemies, but as foul and cruel murderers for whom to die by the sword was too good a fate, and whose only fit end was on the gallows. If they had confined themselves to a revolt against the Government, and in attempting it had slaughtered their officers and all men who tried to suppress it, they would not have placed themselves outside the pale of mercy; but since they had butchered our defenceless women and children, we would have been more than human, we would have been less than men, if we had not exterminated them as men kill snakes whenever we met them. H——well knew that if he did not destroy these sepoys they would destroy him. The slightest hesitation on his part, and they would have sprung to arms, and being caught like rats in a trap, would have fought with the energy of despair. Their muskets against our men's swords would have given their superior numbers a decisive advantage. We should undoubtedly have lost several men, and would probably have been driven back. From this nothing but the prompt and clever strategy adopted by H——saved his party. With all this, it is impossible to avoid a feeling of regret that this incident should have occurred.

V.

CAPTURE OF JHUJJUR.

ONE evening, as my Commanding Officer, Captain Sanford, and I, after dining at mess, returned to the tent which we shared between us, he told me that I need not expect to enjoy that night a very long rest; for he had planned a little expedition on which I was to accompany him. He had got information from a spy of the whereabouts of a small body of the enemy at a village about twelve miles from our camp. He had already given orders for fifty of our men who had been separately and secretly told off to arm themselves and mount their horses as quietly as possible soon after midnight, and sneak out of camp, one by one, through a picquet which had been warned to let them pass. He had taken none of the officers except myself and the Adjutant into his confidence, partly to escape their importunities to be allowed to accompany us, and partly because there was no certainty that we might not be going on a wild goose chase. At the stroke of midnight we arose, dressed and armed ourselves, fortified our stomachs with a cup of hot tea, crammed into our holsters a cold roast fowl apiece and some chapatties, mounted our horses and stole out of camp to the rendezvous, where we found our party and a guide waiting for us. Placing the guide in front under the escort of a couple of sowars, and whispering to the men on the right flank to follow in single file, Sanford noiselessly led the way. Not till we had placed a couple of miles between ourselves and camp did we halt, form up, and "tell off," after which necessary proceeding we continued our journey, stumbling along in the dark over fields and by foot-paths till our guide intimated that we were within a mile of our destination. As it was still an hour or so before dawn we now halted, dismounted, looked to our girths, and loosened our swords in their scabbards. When we again moved on, preceded by a few scouts, with whom was the guide, the very faintest flush of light was beginning to suffuse the sky in the east. In a few minutes more the darkness of night had partially rolled away; and we could see, not far to our front, a group of thatched roofs, and a few tiny curls of blue smoke where some early risers had begun their preparations for breakfast. Almost at the same moment we came across two or three sepoys who had thus early come out into the field. Short shrift had they. We pressed on; and then a carbine shot broke the stillness, followed by the clattering of horses' hoofs, as a small picquet, which—strange to say—had actually been posted on the look-out, took the alarm and galloped away.

After them we went, *ventre a terre*, and drove them right into the village, which turned out to be a small one, and not in any way protected by earthworks. From the complete absence of any attempt at checking us by musketry fire, coupled with the uproar within the hamlet, it was evident that our sudden attack had smitten its defenders with panic; so Sanford with his usual boldness promptly decided to strike while the iron was hot. Detaching two small squads to sweep round the place and join us on the opposite side, he led the main party at a gallop straight up the main street, and through the village, into the fields beyond, which were already full of fugitives. They were all mounted, but many of them had been in such a hurry to bolt that they had not had time to saddle their horses. Though they were two or three times our number, and—if they had kept a really efficient look-out, could easily have beaten us off—they were so completely demoralised by terror that they did not make the slightest effort to rally, but fled in all directions, each man for himself, and each trying to make the fastest time on record. It may be imagined what a holiday this was for our fierce "Guides." Soon was the plain strewn with the bodies of their victims; and though many of the rebels when overtaken used their *tulwars* as well as they could, they only succeeded in slightly wounding a few of our men.

One unfortunate fellow, who fell to my lot, threw himself off his horse when I had nearly overtaken him, and boldly facing me on foot, tried to draw his *tulwar*; but the more he tugged the less would it leave the scabbard. For a moment I thought fear had paralysed his arm; but I discovered afterwards that he had tied his hilt to the scabbard, and in his hurry and very natural agitation had forgotten all about the fastening. It was not at all an unusual practice with native swordsmen to thus fasten up their *tulwars*, with the view of preventing their keen edges from getting blunted by friction.

For three or four miles we kept up the pursuit, when Sanford sounded the "halt" and "rally" and our scattered men gradually obeyed the summons, and assembled, many of them leading captured horses, and laden with loot in the shape of arms and odds and ends, among which were doubtless many gold mohurs and rupees extracted from the *cummerbunds* of the fallen sowars. Very unobtrusive was our return into camp that evening. Not till after dusk did we sneak in as we had sneaked out, by ones and twos; for we were by no means anxious that the General should come to hear of our unsanctioned escapade, till, at any rate, Sanford had found time to think over the most judicious excuse for it.

As we stretched our tired legs under the table in the mess tent, and refreshed our dry throats with a welcome draught of "tarbund" beer, we looked forward to a good night's rest after our day's adventures, for the force was not to resume its march till daylight next morning. At this juncture an official letter was brought by an orderly and handed to the commanding officer, whose face while he read it presented an interesting study. He ended its perusal with a low whistle clearly indicative of puzzled embarrassment; and then communicated its contents to the table. The staff officer of the column had, it seemed, the honour to inform him that the General had received information that a certain village—the very one we had paid our morning call at—was occupied by a strong outpost of the enemy's cavalry. Captain Sanford was desired to take all the available sabres of his regiment and beat up that outpost, timing his march so as, if possible, to effect a surprise about the break of day. In the event of the enemy proving too strong to be dislodged Captain Sanford was to communicate with the General, who would be found on the line of march previously notified in Orders. Here was a pretty dilemma ; what was to be done now ? It would never do at this stage of the affair to report that we had anticipated the General both in information and in acting on it. He would have been furious, so our commanding officer contented himself with acknowledging the receipt of the order. Once more, soon after midnight, we turned out, this time the whole Regiment, some 250 strong ; and marched away in the same direction as on the previous night. Our spirits were not quite so lively as on that occasion, and Sanford was not so gay as usual; for he did not quite see his way out of the scrape he had got into.

At daylight we reached the village, now apparently deserted; and here we met with a wonderful stroke of luck: for in one of the houses we captured a foolish fellow, who, after escaping us the day before, had, thinking the coast was clear, come back in the night to recover some things which he had not had the leisure to pack up before taking his leave. The poor fellow's surprise was painful to witness; but he soon brightened up when he was promised his life on condition that he conducted us to the place where his comrades had taken refuge. This he undertook to do; and, to ensure his fidelity, his hands were securely tied together, and he was mounted on a stray pony, the leading rope of which was given in charge to a couple of men who had orders to shoot him if he attempted to escape.

He said that about six miles further we would find most of his comrades, who had established a bivouac in the open, for they had apparently had enough of village enclosures. His information proved perfectly correct. Directly the enemy saw our scouts they made off in an even greater hurry, if possible, than before. During the pursuit we, as usual, got a good deal scattered. Presently I observed two figures, far away to the left, disappearing into the distance, while behind them, at a long interval, was riding Captain Sanford, followed by a few men. After him I galloped as hard as I could go. When at last I overtook him I found him and his party halted at the gate of a "serai," inside which were about fifty sowars of the Jhujjur troops, with their horses picketed to pegs, and—best prize of all—two light brass guns.

The two figures I had first seen were one of the enemy pursued by a non-commissioned officer of ours who was generally known as the "Shahzada," and who was suspected of not being gifted with an excess of courage. The reader will judge, however, whether the suspicion was well founded. In the pursuit he had singled out one of the enemy, who, being nearly as well mounted as himself, had led him a long chase across country; but he had stuck to him till he ran him to earth in the serai, at the gate of which the Shahzada had to pull up, for it was full of "moofsids." Nothing daunted, he had produced from his belt an enormous horse pistol, covered the lot with it in a general sort of way, informed them that the "Guide Rissala" —name of terror to the rebels—was close at his heels, and threatened to drill a hole into the first man who stirred. The cowardly crew, who had doubtless heard all about the previous day's surprise and slaughter, were too frightened to move. In a few moments Sanford and his men reinforced the Shahzada; and when I rode up were all keeping guard at the gate. Before long we were joined by the main body of the regiment; and then the prisoners were secured; their horses seized; and Sanford, with a light heart, sat down to indite a short despatch to the General, informing him that we had captured fifty prisoners and two brass guns. This was sent off without loss of time; and we commenced our march to rejoin the column; but we were met by an order to stay where we were, as the column would come to us. So we retraced our steps to the serai. Whether Captain Sanford, on the General's arrival, made a clean breast of it, and told him the whole story of the previous day's affair or not, I know not. At any rate, we never heard anything more about it.

A capture of horses was always welcome, for that was the only way in which we could replace casualties among our own mounts; and casualties were pretty frequent in those days from wounds and hard work. We used to select the best of the captives and pass them into the ranks; and sell by auction in camp the others and those whom we rejected from among our own animals. Hitherto we had always considered such prize of war our own perquisites; and no one had interfered with us. It now happened, however, that a levy of mounted police was being raised; and this batch of horses was requisitioned for them. We were, much to our disgust, obliged to part with some of them; but I have a shrewd idea that many of the best remained picketed in our lines. For my own part I was determined to stick to a very handsome roan mare of which I had relieved her former owner, after putting it out of his power to ride her or any other mare any more. Whether the officer to whom the captured animals were to have been made over suspected that some were kept back or exchanged for "screws," I cannot say; but we heard that one of the prisoners was to be sent round our lines to identify them. Before he came the roan mare had been carefully groomed, her mane and tail dressed, my military saddle and bridle fitted on her, and a blanket thrown carelessly over the saddle and her loins. Very charger-like she looked, and very unlike what she had been an hour before. The prisoner when he came on his visit of inspection did not even look at her, but fixed his eyes on a grey Arab, for which I had given a long price some months previously, and after pretending to eye him critically all over, confidently declared that he was one of the captured horses. Such a transparent mistake effectually discredited his evidence; and he was turned out of our lines with ignominy. Many a hard day's work did that roan mare do afterwards; and I daresay she served the State as well when carrying an officer of Irregular Cavalry as she would have done if she had joined the new levy.

That mare was the only "loot" that I allowed myself to take during the Mutiny campaign; and as she was literally the "captive of my bow and spear," in so far as these weapons were represented by a Wilkinson blade, I cannot feel that I was very much to blame for keeping her. On at least one occasion, however, I was sorely tempted. We had taken possession of a deserted town; and our men were busily "searching for arms," a euphemism which covered the quest for many more valuable articles, when I rode into a courtyard under a gate so low that I had to cling to my horse's neck to avoid breaking my own. As I crossed the yard to where a group of my brother officers was standing, one of my horse's feet sunk deep into the ground, which was elsewhere as hard as a stone pavement. This was a sufficient hint to us to dig: and dig we did without delay. Imagine our excitement when, at a depth of two or three feet, we came upon the lid of a large iron chest. Some of our men had been helping us with native spades and hoes which had been left lying about in the huts; and we now placed a couple of them on sentry at the gate to warn off intruders, while we redoubled our labours, and before long had lifted the heavy chest out of its hole. It was locked, and for a time defied all our efforts to break it open. While this was being done, the ever vigilant Father of Evil took advantage of his opportunity.

There could be no doubt that the chest, so carefully hidden, must be full of barbaric gold and gems. Why should we hand all this wealth over to the prize agents? Their operations were confined to Delhi. This village was clearly outside their sphere. They and their employés would never come near it. But for us the chest would never have been discovered. While thoughts such as these were being freely expressed and eagerly discussed the lid of the box was somehow or other forced open; and then was revealed—a mass of documents, quantities of papers bearing revenue stamps, numbers of unused stamps, and absolutely nothing else. These papers, though worthless to us, were yet of great importance and value, as we were informed by the political officers to whom they were made over.

After all "auld Clootie" had not wasted his time. He had succeeded in making some of us feel the power of a good solid temptation; and I daresay had a quiet laugh in his sleeve at our disappointment in not being permitted to succumb to it.

In this same deserted town a certain "Chobdar," a kind of Oriental "gold stick" of the old King's was suspected to be in hiding; and as he was particularly "wanted" by Sir John Metcalfe, the officer in political charge of Delhi, we instituted a very vigorous search for him. A young native lad had been won over by the blandishments of H——to conduct us to a group of huts in one of which he asserted we should surely find the object of our quest. For an hour or more we hunted without success, when, in a small dark room, I noticed one of the large mud-built jars in which natives store their grain. This is, to describe it roughly, a section of a tube closed at both ends, about three feet in diameter and five or six feet high, and stands upright on one end. Near the top a circular hole is cut in the side, into which the grain is poured, and a lid is fitted on to this hole. Possibly Morgiana and the forty thieves flashed across my mind. At any rate I removed the lid, and shoving the muzzle of my revolver into the reservoir, requested its possible occupant to come out. The pistol certainly struck against something which yielded. So I thrust in my arm and caught hold of—a thick beard. A long pull and a strong pull—and out came the Chobdar at full length!

I made him over to my commanding officer, who delivered him up to the political authorities, who, for doubtless sufficient reasons, hanged him on a branch of a tree.

At length came the time when we were to try conclusions with the Nawab of Jhujjur. That rebel Chief was waiting for us at home in his capital, where he had collected a considerable force.

One day, after a long march which had brought our column within a few miles of Jhujjur, we, the Guides Cavalry and a body of Irregular Horse under Captain Pearse, were not a little disgusted by the receipt of orders to retrace our steps at once to a point not far from whence we had just come. To the subaltern mind there seemed no sense in this arrangement; and as our commanding officer did not enlighten us as to the reason for it, we grumbled a good deal as we hurriedly watered and fed our horses, and then started on the weary return march.

Late in the afternoon we had arrived at our destination, and were then warned to be in readiness to march again soon after midnight. Just before dark I had strolled a few hundred yards from camp by myself and was returning, when I was suddenly confronted among some low rolling sandhills by a "sowari" camel carrying two native riders. To present my revolver at them and call on them to halt took about a second; and so taken aback were they that they obeyed at once. I then made them dismount and lead their camel before me to camp. Far better would it have been for them if they had risked my fire and tried to escape; for on them was found a letter which they were carrying to the Jhujjur Nawab, and which contained the news of our movements and a guess at our strength. They paid the penalty which in all wars is exacted from spies. As things turned out their capture were a most fortunate accident; for when, in the darkness of the night, our small force of sabres paraded for the march, we were for the first time informed of the reason for our eccentric movements. It seemed that General Showers intended to attack Jhujjur that morning from the opposite site to that where we were now posted. His having taken us with him and then sent us back was a *ruse de guerre*, the object of which the reader will easily divine. He thought it more than probable that the Nawab and his troops when they were driven out of Jhujjur would—thinking the coast was clear in our direction—take that route to another strong place which lay behind us, and that they would fall into our hands.

We were warned to make as little noise as possible, and were strictly forbidden to smoke. We had a good many miles to cover before getting near Jhujjur, so we moved off in column of route. Shortly before dawn we heard a distant voice gaily singing and gradually becoming louder as it approached us. The minstrel proved to be one of a small party of sowars who must have been the most egregious cowards of the Jhujjur garrison, for they had evidently fled long before any one else; and were doubtless congratulating themselves on their timely escape from the fierce "Feringhis" when to their horror they found themselves in our midst. A few swift flashes of steel and their songs were over for ever.

The day began gradually to break as we pushed eagerly on, meeting at intervals other small parties, of whom not one escaped, though some made a desperate fight for life. At length, just before the sun rose, as we neared the summit of some rising ground which we were ascending, our scouts galloped back with news that the main body of the fugitives was within sight. We at once formed line to the front in rank entire, a formation which I may explain for the benefit of civilian readers, is composed of only one rank instead of two, and which, of course, doubles the extent of front; for our leader wished to frighten the enemy by an imposing show of force, rightly judging that at a distance they would not see that we had no rear rank. Our line advanced to the crest of the high ground, and then burst on our view a sight which can never be forgotten.

A gentle slope stretched away from us, ending in a wide plain which was covered with a huge crowd moving towards us in a disorderly mob. Fighting men on horse-back and on foot—on camels—on a stray elephant or two—in bullock carts and "ekkas"—without any show of discipline or regular formation, mingled with hundreds of non-combatants all pressing tumultuously onwards.

For a moment our long line halted full in view of the enemy. Then rang out the commands "Prepare to draw swords."—"Draw swords." Our sabres flashed into light, gleaming in the rays of the rising sun. "Forward at a walk;" "March;" "Trot;" "Gallop; "Charge." Down the slope we thundered. Like the sands on a dry plain struck by a sudden squall the dense mob before us with a wild cry of despair, broke into fragments and fled—in vain! Our impetus carried us into the midst of them. For miles we pursued them, and heavy was the loss we inflicted on those who bore arms.

Theoretically, cavalry should at all times be kept well in hand and under perfect control. Practically, it would be quite as easy to bind the winds after they had burst out of the bag of Æolus, as to control cavalry once launched in pursuit. What else could possibly be expected? The enemy, if mounted, scatters in flight in all directions, and at racing pace. If they are to be overtaken and destroyed the pursuers also must scatter, and at still greater speed. A very few minutes will cover miles of country with a rapidly extending fan of more or less isolated swiftly-moving groups. Such, at any rate, was our frequent experience during the

Mutiny campaigns. The only remedy would have been to have invariably kept a strong reserve; but this precaution was, with such contemptible antagonists, hardly necessary. After the first few trials of strength the rebels had thoroughly learned the lesson that an encounter with our troops in the open field invariably meant defeat, and that the consequences of defeat were terrible. Having no real discipline or organisation, and no confidence in their leaders, they always met us with what may be best described as nervous hesitation; and their promptitude in bolting was often astonishing. Frequently would individuals and small knots of men turn to bay and fight manfully; but usually not till they also had yielded to the general impulse of panic, and had joined for a time in the stampede.

In this pursuit I had the good fortune to kill a mutineer who must undoubtedly have been concerned in the murder of some European, for I found on him a gold mourning ring bearing on the circlet, in black enamelled letters, the words "In memory of." The stone, which evidently must have been inscribed with some name, was missing. The wretch made no fight, but died like a cur, with my blade through his back. Observing that his *cummurbund* bulged considerably, I unrolled it; and out of its folds fell a quantity of rupees and other things, among which was the ring, which I took, leaving the rest of the loot for any one who might be inclined to pick it up. I placed the ring on one of my fingers, resolving, when the opportunity should offer, to have a bloodstone inserted in it, with the date 1857.

To my great regret, later in the day, I found that the ring, which was rather loose for my finger, had slipped off it, and was lost.

It will be admitted that when we joined the rendezvous at Jhujjur we had, during the past forty-eight hours, done a fair share of work; but more was in store for us. The Nawab was a prisoner in the hands of the General, who decided to send him without delay to head-quarters at Delhi; and we were ordered to escort him. Accordingly in the afternoon the Nawab, who was a heavy, corpulent man, was placed in a doolie provided with a large number of bearers; and once more our tired horses were on the move. I forget what was the distance between Jhujjur and Delhi; but I well remember that the march was a very long and fatiguing one; and that it was not before the dawn of next day that we had finished it, and were able to hand our prisoner over to other custodians.

He was duly tried, found guilty, and hanged in the Chandni Chowk, the principal street of Delhi.

VI.

EN ROUTE FOR LUCKNOW.

About this time I seized an opportunity of getting a few days' leave to run over to Meerut. Soon after my return the Corps of Guides which, since its arrival in the camp before Delhi after its famous forced march from the far frontier, had continuously rendered services not eclipsed by any other troops which had the honour to take part in the siege, received orders to return to Hoti Murdan. Its losses, both in the cavalry and infantry branches of the regiment, had been so numerous that it became absolutely necessary to fill their places with recruits.

To my deep sorrow my connection with this distinguished regiment then came to an end; but while I live it will always be a source of pride to me to have been privileged to serve with it, even for so short a time, during the memorable siege of Delhi.

Though Delhi had fallen and the Punjab was secure, the revolt was yet far from having been suppressed in the Provinces of the North-West and Oudh. There was still plenty of service to be seen in those parts; and I was naturally anxious to find my way down to them. In those days it was fortunately not very difficult to get to the front when any fighting was to be done. There was work for every one, and plenty of it. Since then, many a keen soldier not possessed of influential friends at head-quarters, has had to be content to find himself shut out from the series of "little wars," so prolific of medals and decorations and brevet promotion, which seem providentially provided for the swift advancement in the service of his more fortunate comrades who are equipped with that best of military qualifications —"interest."

Not to digress, however, the opportunity was afforded me of getting transferred to the 1st Sikh Irregular Cavalry, a corps which had been newly raised in the Punjab by the late Captain Wale, and was commanded by him; and which about this time arrived at Delhi *en route* to join Sir Colin Campbell's forces in the south. That regiment began, under Wale, a distinguished career which it continued under Probyn in China. It is now the 11th Prince of Wales's Own Bengal Lancers, and still maintains its high reputation among the many splendid regiments which compose the Bengal and Punjab Cavalry; a force of horsemen which, it is safe to say, is not excelled, as regards all the best qualities of light cavalry, by any troops in the world.

If the smart 11th Bengal Lancers could see themselves as they appeared when, as the 1st Sikh Irregulars, they marched down the grand trunk road from Delhi in the winter of 1857, they would be not a little amused and astonished. Every variety of bit, bridle, saddle *tulwar*—every variety of horse, entire, mare, and gelding,—of all heights, from 15 hands to animals little bigger than ponies. Such were the equipment and the mounting of the regiment; and our notions of drill were at first equally primitive. It was all we could do to "form threes right" or "left." The men, however—if no two of them rode alike, and none of them had a "cavalry seat"—were undeniable horsemen; and there was never any difficulty in getting them, when an enemy was before them, to form some sort of a line to the front, and to ride as hard and as straight, if not with quite as good "dressing," as the better drilled troops of the present day.

On our first march from Delhi a comical incident, which, however, might easily have turned out rather a serious one, occurred. I was riding with the advanced files, when a young native woman, wielding with both hands a very long straight double-edged sword, such as is frequently used by acrobats at Indian festivities, suddenly appeared in the middle of the road and barred our way. The creature must have been mad or under the influence of "bhang" or some other intoxicant; for she deluged us with a torrent of abuse as she vigorously brandished the long thin blade. For a moment I was nonplussed : the situation was so entirely novel ! Mad or sane, the virago evidently meant business. There was clearly no getting past her without a fight; and that was quite out of the question.

"Shoot her, sahib," said one of the sowars with me, little troubled with the polite consideration for the sex which the obligations of an effete civilisation imposed upon his British officer. At that moment, as if by inspiration, a "happy thought" flashed on my mind. "Give her *galee*" (abuse) I said to the sowar ; "and give it her hot and strong, and plenty of it." Instantly grasping the idea, the grinning sowar opened such a battery of abuse of the vilest and most comprehensive nature upon the unfortunate young person and her female relatives to the remotest degree that her own fire was promptly silenced. Encouraged by this success, the sowar redoubled his efforts; and slung such awful and shameful language with such force and precision that the rout of the enemy speedily became complete. Dropping her long sword and stuffing her fingers into her ears, she fled with a horrified shriek; and we marched triumphantly on, chuckling at the success of our tactics.

Nothing very exciting occurred during the long, dusty march to Cawnpore. For a considerable part of the way we had to escort an immense train of empty bullock carts, destined for the use of Sir Colin's army; and our duties were monotonous in the extreme. Heartily would we have welcomed an attack on our convoy; but none was ever made.

At Cawnpore I was left in command of a detachment of fifty sabres, while the head-quarters of the regiment went on to Alumbagh, near Lucknow. This was a grievous disappointment to me; but as things turned out, nothing more lucky could have happened.

After having marched here and there about the country with a column under Brigadier-General Cardew, during which time nothing worth record occurred, we returned to Cawnpore and remained there for a while. My comrade and fellow-subaltern at that time was Lieutenant now (Colonel) Sir Robert Sandeman, *K. C. S. I.*, to whose wisdom and tact and perseverance India owes her present impregnable frontier on the North-West, and the gradual conversion of the wild tribes of Baluchistan into friendly and peaceful communities. He and I one day rode out to visit our friends, the 3rd Battalion of the Rifle Brigade, at Unao, on the Lucknow road, where they were encamped under the command of Colonel Macdonell. While there the Colonel took me aside and informed me that a messenger had just come in with an urgent request for help from a village some few miles to the north, which was held by a small detachment of police. The village which, like most others in Oudh at that date, was fortunately protected by a strong and lofty mud-built wall, was attacked by a force of some hundreds of rebels; and unless speedily relieved its defenders were in danger of running short of ammunition. It was promptly arranged that Sandeman and I should gallop back to Cawnpore, report the state of affairs to General Sir John Inglis, and obtain his permission to bring our detachment as quickly as possible across country to a point about three miles from the threatened post, where we were to join a couple of companies of the Rifle Brigade and proceed to its relief.

Off we set as fast as our horses could carry us. It was late in the evening when we arrived; Sandeman going straight to our lines to turn out our men, while I went to the Fort and obtained an interview with Sir John Inglis.

He was at first apparently disinclined to let so young an officer take a detachment at night so far from support into the wilds; but at last he listened to my arguments, and after impressing on me that I was to act under the orders of Colonel Macdonell, allowed me to go.

When I got to the lines I found the men already mounted and "told off," and fresh horses ready for Sandeman and myself: so that we got under way at once. After crossing the bridge of boats we struck across country in a slanting direction to the left of the road. Night had fallen, but we had the advantage of a certain amount of moonlight, and were able to move pretty rapidly. When we arrived at the rendezvous there were no signs of Colonel Macdonell or his rifles; but a letter from him was put into my hands by a native messenger, who said that the Colonel, after starting from Unao, had gone back there on hearing that at nightfall the rebels had raised the siege of the village, and had retired to another some miles away. This after our long journey to Cawnpore and back was a terrible disappointment.

Possibly, however, the Colonel might have thought it undesirable to follow the enemy so great a distance with infantry, and might wish me to do so with my troop. The thought no sooner struck me than its "sweet reasonableness" began to grow on me; and I had very soon persuaded myself that the yet unopened missive contained instructions which chimed with my wishes. Unfortunately, however, it was too dark to read the letter without a light, and I had no matches! Neither, very curiously, had Sandeman! At any rate, we did not find any in our pockets: so we held a short council of war; and decided that in the absence of instructions, we felt it our duty to proceed to the lately beleaguered village, and learn all we could about the movements of the enemy. We took the messenger with us as a guide, and in another hour had reached our destination.

The brave defenders were delighted to see us; but they informed us that the rebels had not gone far, and would certainly return in the morning; and they implored us not to leave them to their fate.

On inquiring how many fighting men they could muster, we found that they could turn out about a hundred muskets and matchlocks of sorts. I then asked them what they thought was the strength of the enemy. About five or six hundred they said. Allowing for Oriental exaggeration, we guessed that two hundred and fifty or three hundred would probably be nearer the mark; so I asked them if they were game to accompany us and beat up their late assailants, whom we would certainly find quite unprepared for our midnight visit. With the greatest alacrity they agreed: so, without loss of time, I made my dispositions, and formed up my little army in the order which it was to keep till the moment of attack. In the centre I managed with some difficulty to get the police and the armed villagers to arrange themselves in a line, impressing on them that if they could keep that formation till we came in contact with the enemy, they would certainly be mistaken for a company of the dreaded *gora logue* (white troops), which would be a heavy score in our favour. My own party I divided into two bodies of 25 sabres each and placed one on each flank, giving the command of the left to Lieutenant Sandeman and of the right to a native officer, till the moment of the charge, when I proposed to lead it. I then explained the plan ot attack, and took very good care that every man of my motley allies thoroughly understood it, and appreciated the extreme necessity of adhering to it. A guide was placed in front of the centre of the line, where I took up my position; and he was ordered to lead me straight to the camp of the rebels, who, we were assured, would be found "en bivouac" close to a village about three miles away. The very strictest silence was enjoined on all. As my object was to surprise the enemy and fall on him without giving him the slightest hint of our approach, I did not send forward a single scout. The line was to advance quietly and steadily, till I should give a loud "Hurrah," which was to be the signal for the police and village heroes to "loose off" every musket they had, and to yell with all their lungs, when the cavalry from both flanks would charge, also with a shout.

If all that did not freeze the marrow in the bones of a lot of sleepy Pandies, I flattered myself nothing would!

So we moved off over the fields—the soft earth muffling all sound—my improvised infantry keeping a really wonderful line—and all as eager as panthers.

In an hour or so the guide whispered to me that we were close on our quarry, but nothing was to be seen. The night, though not pitch-dark, was sufficiently so to obscure all objects beyond thirty or forty yards. Most fortunately a belt of trees was now behind us, which must have effectually prevented us from being seen from our front. Suddenly I became aware of the *silhouette* of a man's figure against the sky of the horizon before me, slowly moving, apparently along the top of a low wall. Almost at the same instant from the dim figure came a loud challenge:—"Hookumdar!" He must have been startled by some sound, for he could not have seen us.

I held my breath, for I feared that my villagers might get excited, and spoil my plans by beginning to fire; but they behaved admirably and crept steadily on. Now we were within forty yards of the sentry. "Hookumdar!" he shouted again. For a few yards more we crouched forward, when the sentry, now thoroughly alarmed, once more roared "Hookumdar," and fired his musket. Now was the moment! I gave the signal "Hurrah" as loud as my lungs would let me, and galloped off to my squad of sowars, while the line of villagers simultaneously let off all their fire-arms, and burst into an uproar of wild yells to which the worst efforts of a pack of mad jackals would have been a feeble joke.

A few seconds covered the ground between us and the rebel bivouac, and brought us up to a shallow ditch and a low wall, which, though they brought down one or two of our horses, did not for a moment check the furious charge. So complete was the surprise and so utterly unprepared for, that beyond a few scattered musket shots fired off harmlessly in panic, not the very slightest effort at a stand was made. The wretched Pandies as they jumped up, half dazed with sleep, from the ground and off the charpoys on which they had been lying, must have been utterly bewildered by the fiendish yells and the roar of musketry which for many of them was their last "reveille;" and they fled helter-skelter in all directions into the fields, pursued and mercilessly slain by the Sikh horsemen, whose scanty numbers their fears must have magnified a hundredfold. Some were actually sabred on the ground before they were well awake. Others were caught before they had got a dozen yards away; and in a few minutes the surrounding fields were covered with the bodies of many more; while the lucky survivors, favoured by the darkness, made off at best speed to unknown and distant parts, and doubtless had a gruesome tale to unfold when at last they reached some safe asylum, as to how they had escaped by the favour of God and by the skin of their teeth, after performing prodigies of unavailing valour, from a midnight attack by the whole British army.

The darkness made it inadvisable to push the pursuit very far, more especially as the defeat of the rebels was so decisive that there was practically no danger of their recovering from it and making any effort to rally, and it was very certain that they would not for some time trust themselves in our part of the country, far less attempt to renew the attack on the police outpost. So I re-assembled the troop, and was happy to find that beyond a few trifling scratches we had incurred no casualties whatever.

We now contrived to read Colonel Macdonell's letter, and found that its contents were not exactly what we had persuaded ourselves they might be. The Colonel had in fact desired me to return to camp at Cawnpore, since the voluntary retirement of the besiegers from the threatened village had put an end to the object of our expedition. However, to use a homely phrase, there is no help for spilt milk. What we had done could not be undone, so we decided to finish the job in a workmanlike manner. To this end we collected in heaps such property as had been abandoned by the enemy, and made bonfires of it. We also destroyed by fire the neighbouring fortified village which had harboured them, and which it was most fortunate they were not occupying when we arrived on the scene; for it stood on high ground, and we should have found it a hard nut to crack. It was delightful to witness the exuberant joy and vainglorious excitement of our valiant matchlockmen; and we all marched back in the best of spirits to their home, now released from danger; where we left them to enjoy the congratulations of their womenfolk, while we continued our journey back to Cawnpore—a journey which turned out to be not entirely without adventure.

We had, of course, secured a guide; and for some few miles we marched quietly on, when, judging that we could easily find our way to the bridge over the river by the position of the moon and stars, Sandeman and I, taking an orderly with us, left the party to follow leisurely while we trotted on, for I was anxious to report our success to Sir John Inglis as speedily as possible; but we had not gone more than a mile or two when the sky became so thickly overcast with clouds that not only was the darkness intensified, but our beacons were lost to view. We had to fall into a walk, and very cautiously did we move; for if we did unfortunately lose the proper direction there was no certainty that we might not fall in with a stray camp of the enemy, who at that time infested the district.

Presently we came in sight of a number of twinkling lights, and held a debate as to whether we should make for them or not. We decided, however, that it would be prudent to avoid them, so we moved on in the opposite direction; and after a while came across a small hamlet, the watchful dogs of which all commenced to bark in chorus. Into the village we trotted at a smart pace, and finding a man asleep on a "charpoy" outside his hut, we roused him up, and started him at a run out of the place and into the open fields almost before he had time to wake. We then explained matters to him and offered him a reward if he conducted us safely to the bridge, with the alternative of something quite different if he led us into any trap.

We found that we had, after all, come pretty straight, and were within a mile or two of the river. At the bridge we dismissed our guide with the promised reward; and as dawn was now breaking I went on to the Fort and sought the General's quarters, not without trepidation; for now that cool reflection had time to sit in judgment on hot impulse, I was not quite certain in what light our proceedings would strike that redoubtable officer, and what measure of allowance he would make for the rather lame excuse which I had to offer for not having obeyed Colonel Macdonell's instructions. I began to have grave doubts as to whether he would swallow the match story; and I heartily wished the interview well over.

Sir John gravely listened to my report and then proceeded to administer a "wigging" which took all the conceit out of me, and made me wish that I had passed the previous night quietly in my bed instead of in hunting rebels in the jungle. My twitching face must have betrayed the acuteness of my pain, for the kind old General, laying his hand on my shoulder, went on to say something to the following effect:—"Don't be too much upset about this. As your General I was bound to rebuke you; for if by any chance you had failed instead of succeeded—if your party had lost many lives and had been repulsed into the bargain—you would have got into serious trouble. As things have turned out all has gone well, and you have read these Pandies an excellent lesson; and, in fact, I am not really at heart displeased with you. Perhaps I may find you another job some day soon."

If a condemned criminal were reprieved at the scaffold, and were presented with a handsome fortune into the bargain, his feelings would be like mine at that moment.

The promised job turned up not very long afterwards.

I was directed to take my troop to a point on the river several miles above Cawnpore, and to establish a series of picquets along its course for the purpose of frustrating any attempt on the part of the rebels to cross it. To assist me in this duty a considerable body of newly-raised semi-military police was placed at my disposal, and I was told that I could thoroughly rely on their fidelity. As the length of front which I had to guard stretched for many miles, it was clear that my fifty sabres could do little in the way of furnishing picquets. I therefore made the following dispositions. At favourable points along the river I established a chain of small police posts, of about ten men, each under a non-commissioned officer. Further inland, on the lines of radii leading to my own position, I placed three parties of my own men, each consisting of a duffadar and three sowars.

The rest of the detachment I kept together at a central point a mile or two from the river. The duties of the police posts were to keep an incessant and vigilant look-out, and to patrol the banks, keeping touch with each other. In the event of any suspicious movements being observed on the opposite side of the river, or of any attempt to cross it anywhere, they were at once to communicate with the nearest of my connecting links, who would forward the information to me; and I should thus be always able to move the main body of my detachment promptly to any threatened point. Sandeman and I took it in turns to visit the whole of the picquets—a duty which entailed a ride of between twenty and thirty miles. Having made these arrangements I felt quite easy in my mind, and waited on events. For some time, however, no attempt at evading our vigilance was made.

One morning I was informed that the day was a sort of religious festival, on which a certain rebel Raja, whose territory was on the other side of the river, was accustomed to come with a considerable following to the bank for the purpose of bathing in State; so Sandeman and I betook ourselves to the police post opposite which the "tamasha" was expected to take place. At that point the river was over a thousand yards wide, far beyond the range of any weapons possessed by us, with the exception of a double-barrelled Lancaster oval smoothbore of my own, whose powers I proposed to try if I got the chance. I then procured a couple of "charpoys," and sat upon one while I rigged the other up in front of it, placing it upright on one of its sides in such a manner as to afford an excellent and steady rest for my rifle. Presently a couple of elephants with howdahs on their backs, and surrounded by the usual rag-tag and bobtail which in those days was inseparable from a native magnate, emerged from some trees on the other side of the river, and slowly moved down to it with much waving of "chowries" and beating of "tom-toms."

While the elephants were splashing in the water I drew a bead on the biggest of them, and fired. The bullet sped through the air. Whether it hit the elephant or not I cannot say; but the effect of its arrival on the hitherto festive scene was quite ludicrous. With one accord did both elephants and their attendants turn tail and scamper out of the water, and up the bank into the shelter of the trees, followed by a messenger from the other barrel, which I despatched to hasten their movements. The angry Raja now replied to my insults with half-a-dozen matchlock bullets, which fell harmlessly into the water about half way across; but he did not venture to resume his interrupted bath, and very soon departed *re infecta.*

After he had gone I observed a couple of large "country" boats lying under the opposite bank, and offered a reward to some villagers if they would go across and get them, while I promised to drive off with the rifle, whose wonderful range they had just witnessed, any assailants who might try to interfere with them. A few manjees (boatmen) volunteered for the job, and, by wading in shallow parts and swimming in deeper ones, soon succeeded in crossing the river, each of them taking with him a long bamboo pole. They took possession of the boats without being molested, and had got them half way across to our side when a few matchlock men appeared, running along beside the river and firing at them. A couple of shots from the Lancaster, however, very quickly persuaded them to take themselves out of its reach; and the boats were at length safely moored under the protection of the police picquet.

It was not often that anything of interest happened, and the days sometimes passed rather monotonously. On such occasions we would occasionally beguile the time by getting one or other of the native officers or men to relate their adventures when fighting against "the Sirkar," which many of them had done at Moodkee, Chillianwalla, Sobraon, and many another famous field, when the brave troops of the Khalsa covered themselves with glory, and earned from their British antagonists the respect which all soldiers entertain for "foemen worthy of their steel."

One of the stories we thus heard fixed itself on my memory, and I will endeavour to reproduce it. The narrator, a fine sturdy old Sikh gentleman, had been persuaded to divulge the history of each of the honourable scars which adorned his body, with the exception of one which crossed the bridge of his nose, and rather spoiled its symmetry. On my asking him whether that wound also was a memento of war, he replied :—"Ah, Sahib! I cannot tell you that story. You would be angry with me." "Angry with you," I said, "why should I be angry if, as I suppose, you got the wound in honest fight against us? Even if you killed the man who inflicted it, that was his luck. What is it to me? Come! Tell us all about it." "Very well, Sahib, if you wish it and will promise not to think the worse of me, I will tell you. This is how it was. You have heard of the great battle at Chillianwalla, and you know how fierce it was, and how stoutly the Sikhs of the Khalsa fought that day. The Sirkar Angrez* claims the victory; but believe me, Sahib, we won that fight. Did not the Jungie Lat Sahib† retire from the field after the battle? Did not we capture four of your guns and the standards of three of your regiments? Did not our horsemen overthrow the Gora regiment and the Hindustani risala? Forgive me, Sahib; but that is true; and if Shere Singh had, next day, pushed his advantage, and had boldly attacked the shaken troops of the Sirkar, he must have driven them clean out of the Punjab. At

* English Government.

† Commander-in-Chief.

that time I was—as I am now—a Sirdar; and commanded a tolee* of infantry of my own people. At a certain moment of the battle we found ourselves opposed at close quarters to a British battalion, which the fury of our fire had temporarily checked: but if they hesitated, so did we. In vain did I call on my men to throw away their muskets, and rush, sword in hand, to the attack. Neither line dared advance; and neither would retire; and there we knelt—for a dreadful minute or two—pouring a frightful hail of fire into each other at less than a hundred yards. Both sides were actually melting away under it. Such fearful stress could not possibly last. One or other line was certain to give way. Whichever had the courage to rush forward first was sure to win. Frantic were the efforts of the officers of the Gora logue to urge on their men; but in vain. Nothing could get them to move. Suddenly a young officer—so young—he was but a smoothfaced, rosy-cheeked but-

* Squad.

cha'*—got beside himself with excitement, and waving over his head his foolish little 'Regulation' blade, and shouting 'Hurrah!' 'Hurrah!' he sprang forward quite alone, and flew at me like a madman; and almost before I could see what he was doing, smote me across the face. Poor boy! What could I do! If I had not protected myself he would have run me through the body with his thin spit of a sword. So I had to smite with my keen tulwar, and smite hard. Next moment the Gora logue were upon us, roaring like tigers, and we were swept away before them. I remember the rush, the clash of steel, and then nothing more. I became *behosh*.† When I recovered my senses I found my head bleeding, and a great lump on the top of it; but no other wound except the cut on my nose. I suppose I must have been knocked down by a clubbed musket. Night had fallen, and the field was deserted except by the dead and dying,

* Youngster. | † Senseless.

and by gangs of plunderers. I stumbled along for a *kos* or two, helped by some of our own people whom I met on the way; and then I found myself once more in safety in the camp of Shere Singh. You are not angry, Sahib! What could I do? That boy would have killed me. Every one must protect his own life."

Thus, with mingled grief and pride, did we listen to the story of how "somebody's darling" had died for his country's honour.

VII.

DILKHOOSHA.

WHILE we lay in that camp keeping guard over the river we were joined by another young officer, and an incident occurred to all three of us which was, to say the least, mysterious. Our *bawarchi*, or cook, was a Hindustani Musalman, and we had every reason to be satisfied with his culinary performances, till one morning after breakfast, when both of my companions who had sat down to that meal in perfect health and with hearty appetites, suffered from sudden nausea. As I was not similarly affected, and had eaten the same food with them, it did not occur to us to suspect foul play. However, the same thing happened more than once; and at last, on one occasion, we were all three violently sick almost immediately after our morning repast. This was altogether too suspicious: so, since a careful inspection of our copper pots and

THE RESIDENCY, LUCKNOW.

pans showed that they were not in fault, having been recently tinned, we came to the conclusion that an attempt was being made to poison us. Here was a pretty state of affairs. If we dismissed the *bawarchi* it was hopeless to think of getting a substitute for him. We should have had to starve, or trust to the hospitality of our men for *chapatties*, such as they themselves eat. Something had to be done, however, and this is what we did. A sentry was placed over the cook during the time that he was engaged in preparing our food, and he was ordered to keep a sharp eye on that individual, and to confiscate and bring to me any condiment or other material which he might propose to use that was not manifestly harmless. These were not the orders which the cook thought were given to the sentry. He was, with much emphasis, given to understand that the Sikh who stood over him with a naked *tulwar* had been directed to smite off his head the moment he detected any suspicious act; and as he knew that nothing would please the grim disciple of Nanuk better than to carry out such instructions at the expense of a follower of the Arabian Prophet, his lot at once ceased to be a happy one. In fact, it was very much the reverse, and it became quite interesting to observe his proceedings under the terror of the sword of Damocles, which now hung over him. With his sleeves carefully rolled up above his elbows he squatted before the three small sloping hollows in the ground with sides and backs of stones, which formed his kitchen range, and carried on his operations in fear and trembling; for close behind him stood the vigilant Sikh. Whenever he glanced upwards he could not avoid seeing the blue steel of the sharp curved blade; and sometimes the sentry, willing to amuse himself, would frown wickedly, and peer into a *degchi* as if he detected something wrong. At such critical moments the wretched creature would fairly grin with fright, as with chattering teeth and supplicating hands he resigned himself to the worst.

Then would the scowling Sikh growl out a gruff *khabardar!** and tell him to go on with his work.

Our suspicions may have been unjust; and the fact may have been only a coincidence. Nevertheless it *was* a fact that no more unpleasant symptoms attacked any of us after our meals. On the whole, we thought it fair to give the cook the benefit of the doubt; and we seized the first opportunity of dispensing with his services.

We were beginning to flatter ourselves that the watch on the Ganges kept by our police auxiliaries was altogether too stringent for the enterprise of the rebels; but we were mistaken. It so happened that one morning Sandeman and I rode round the picquets together. For some distance all was apparently quiet on the river; and no report of anything unusual was made by any of the police posts. We had just arrived close to one of them, when to our astonishment we suddenly came upon the broad and fresh

* Beware.

track of a considerable number of horses and camels, clearly marked on the soft wet soil, and leading inland from the river straight past and immediately under the high ground on which the picquet was posted. We could hardly believe our eyes. It was quite clear that within a few hours a crossing had been effected by some two or three hundred mounted men, right under the noses of the police, upon whose fidelity I had been instructed to rely, and who had carefully concealed the fact from me, if they had not actively aided the rebels. As soon as we struck the trail we followed it across the sand to the point where it emerged from the river, which at that point was not very wide. We were immediately greeted by a musket shot from a man half-concealed among the rushes on the opposite shore, and who must have been a very indifferent marksman, for he missed us. As he repeated his performance in less time than he could possibly have reloaded, we judged that another musket must have been handed to him by a confederate more effectually hidden than himself; and as we could not tell how many more might be skulking in the thick cover, we considered it expedient to retire from his neighbourhood, after having replied to his civilities with our revolvers, of course ineffectually. We then went up to the police post, and my first step was to disarm and make prisoners of the whole eleven men composing it; for their treachery was self-evident, and demanded no further enquiry.

There was a large village near by, and in it we found a man suffering from a gun-shot wound, which he said had been wantonly inflicted by one of the rebels as they passed the place early that morning. This was corroborated by other inhabitants of the village, so I considered myself justified in desiring the chief local representative of civil authority, who styled himself a Tahsildar, to accompany me to our camp, where I proposed to take care of him till higher authority should enquire into the propriety of his conduct in not sending me word of what had happened.

In the meantime I wrote with a pencil on some leaves torn out of my note book a short report to Sir John Inglis, commanding at Cawnpore, in which I detailed the circumstances proving the treachery of the police, and suggested that, if possible, they should be replaced by a military force. I also stated that since it was quite evident, both from the appearance of the track and from the testimony of the villagers, that the crossing had been effected in the early dawn, I considered it useless to make any attempt to pursue the party of rebels, who were said to be under the leadership of the Bala Rao, and to be making for Calpee, a place which, having several hours' start, they must already have nearly reached. I concluded by asking for orders as to the disposal of my prisoners; and sent off the despatch at once to Cawnpore.

On our way to camp the Tahsildar met with an accident, which, though serious enough at the time, very possibly saved his neck. He was riding a vicious country-bred over whom he had very imperfect control, and who backed into my horse with the result of causing a violent kicking match, at the end of which the unfortunate man found himself on the broad of his back on the ground with a broken leg. I jumped off, and found that both bones were broken half way between the knee and the ankle. No medical aid was available nearer than Cawnpore; so I had to do the best I could for him on the spot. I therefore cut some stems of *bajra*, or some similar crop which was growing close by; and then, placing myself on the ground before him and getting a purchase with one foot against his body, I laid hold of the injured limb by the ankle and hauled on it with all my strength till I had got the broken surfaces opposite each other, where other hands placed them in position. A portion of his turban was now wrapped next the skin, then a number of the sticks were laid close together all round the leg, and kept fast by cords; and we had rough and ready splints, which answered their purpose admirably. The patient was now carried on a *charpoy* back to his own house, where, after many days, he was seen to by a medical officer who dressed the limb in orthodox fashion, and who declared the original operation had been perfectly successful. I never heard that this Tahsildar had been hanged, as I have little doubt he would have been, if compassion for his crippled condition had not prevented me from pressing the case against him. The ten police men and their *Thanadar* were not so fortunate. A special officer was sent out by Sir John Inglis with full power to enquire into and dispose of their case. To him I explained the arrangements which I had made for watching the river. I showed him the track of the rebel party where it passed within fifty yards of the picquet. His investigation was over in an hour; and at the end of it he sentenced the whole eleven culprits to suffer death as the reward of their treason, and hanged them on one tree. He also informed me that he would report that all my arrangements had been judicious, and that no blame could attach to me or my men.

No further attempt was made by the rebels to cross the river; and indeed none would have been practicable, for General Walpole's Brigade had been moved up the road from Cawnpore, and effectually blocked the way. My party was, however, not relieved; but was allowed to remain where it was; and, as the days rolled on, seemed likely to become a fixture. We began to be apprehensive that we might be overlooked altogether, while preparations were being made by Sir Colin Campbell for the final advance upon Lucknow—a prospect that was far from pleasing—but it was not easy to see how it could be averted. In this perplexity I sought counsel from the Colonel of a regiment which passed our camp on its way to Cawnpore, and who, with some of his officers, lunched with us. He advised me to write to Major-General Mansfield, the Chief of the Staff, and bring our existence to his notice, telling him how long we had been detached from the regiment, which was now at the Alumbagh, and which would, if we were allowed to rejoin it, obtain an accession to its strength of three British officers and fifty sabres. "You will certainly get a wigging," said he, "but it is just possible that your party is really overlooked, and that your letter may effect what you wish. At any rate, a bold horseman must sometimes ride for a fall, if he hopes to get over a stiff place."

I thankfully took his advice and acted on it, and I certainly got the fall he had anticipated; for in due course came an oblong official letter from a staff officer of the Chief of the Staff—not by any means from the great man himself. In that document I was very deservedly rebuked for my presumption in having written direct to the Chief of the Staff, who, I was informed, was not in the habit of corresponding with junior subalterns as to the movements of their detachments. This "awful warning" I pinned conspicuously on the cloth wall of my tent, where to my mingled amusement and trepidation it was soon afterwards seen by the very officer who had written it. Whatever he may have thought of my flippant treatment of his effusion, he made no remarks, and shortly thereafter my detachment was relieved from its post and ordered back to Cawnpore. There I had the good fortune to be attached to the cavalry of Sir Colin Campbell's army, and to march with it towards Lucknow; and such was my luck that, on the 2nd March 1858, when the Commander-in-Chief attacked and captured the high ground at Dilkhoosha dominating the City, I actually found myself in command of the advanced party of the advanced guard; for that was the position of my troop that day. Immediately in rear of it was a squadron of the 9th Lancers, followed by more cavalry and by horse artillery. As we passed the Alumbagh where the head-quarters of our regiment were encamped, I well remember how delighted I felt to think that after all we had stolen a march upon it, and that—not to count that midnight affair near Unao—our troop was to have the honour of being the first to go into action. Well also do I remember the wistful look on the face of my gallant commanding officer, the late Captain Wale, as he watched us pass, and wished us good luck. We all knew that a fight was before us; and it did seem uncommonly hard on the regiment that, after having so long been posted at the very front, it should at the last moment be left, "*planté la,*" by a detachment which had, so to speak, sneaked up from the rear.

When the head of the column had got about midway between the Alumbagh and Dilkhoosha a halt was sounded; and we took the opportunity of making a rapid breakfast of such eatables as we had stowed away in our holsters. During this period a disagreeable drizzling shower of rain did what it could to damp our spirits as well as our bodies; but when we again moved on it had ceased; having laid the dust for us, and given us a cool, pleasant day fit for a review.

Cautiously and steadily we felt our way, covered by half the troop in extended order, commanded by Lieutenant Sandeman, who summarily brushed out of our road sundry small bodies of hostile horsemen whom he encountered. My half troop was in support, and when the skirmishing began we pushed on and joined in the fun. Through orchards and plantations with occasional open fields an intermittent series of little fights was kept up as we continued our advance.

Suddenly, just as we emerged from a grove of trees on to an open plain, a distant puff of smoke followed by a loud report and then by the well-known hoarse hiss of a round shot as it tore through the air above us, gave unmistakable notice that the ball had begun. Another shot fell short, hit the ground in front of us, and then ricoched over our heads to the rear. Another and another in quick succession passed harmlessly. While this was going on I had instinctively taken ground to the right to make room for the troops which I knew would be pushed forward. The squadron of the 9th Lancers followed my example—a troop of horse artillery thundered up from the rear—more cavalry galloped out to the left of the guns—and, like magic, a line was formed to the front, the guns in the centre, with cavalry on both flanks. A trumpet sounded the " advance," and the "gallop," and away we swept over the plain, straight for the enemy's position, under a furious fire, too furious and rapid, fortunately, to do us much mischief. One round shot smote a man of the 9th Lancers full in the face. His head disappeared into space. In a few moments we were within a hundred yards of the enemy, still frantically blazing away at us. Here we came to a halt; and our own guns, with the astonishing swiftness which is the admiration of all other branches of the army, unlimbered and came into action. Very different was their practice from that of the rebel artillery. Equally rapid, but with calm regularity, working like parts of a perfect machine, gun after gun, carefully and accurately laid, pounded away at the opposing battery, and with almost instantaneously overpowering effect. A very few rounds, and the fire of the enemy slackened away, and soon nearly ceased altogether.

While this artillery duel was going on I had a good opportunity of observing the effect of what is popularly known as "blue funk" on a young recruit. He was in the rear rank; and while the excitement of galloping to the front lasted, had kept his place among his comrades; but to sit still within a hundred yards of guns belching out smoke and noise and round shot was more than his nerves were equal to; and he began—half unconsciously, I daresay—to pull on his horse's head and gradually back him out of the ranks. This would never do! Example is catching, so I galloped round behind him and used language calculated to bring him to his senses, but without effect. With his mouth half-open and his eyes starting out of his head he continued to stare at the terrifying guns, greeting each explosion with a horrified little groan; and all the time he kept backing his horse on to me. I was obliged to put an end to this. In another moment he would have bolted and disgraced us all—possibly infected some of his comrades with his own panic. For the last time I shouted that I would run my sword into him if he did not "dress up." He took no heed; and I lunged at him with all my force. His luck saved him. He had a small buffalo-hide buckler hanging from his left shoulder; and instinctively he twisted half round and caught the point of my sword in it, and there it stuck. The more I pulled and the worse language I used, the less would it come out; and I am afraid the string of words with which I expressed my disgust must have been far from discreetly chosen, when behind me a voice exclaimed:—

THE BAILEY GUARD GATE, LUCKNOW.

"Who commands this party?" Looking round, the unfortunate recruit's panic was nothing to what mine became, when I saw the stern face of the Commander-in-Chief, Sir Colin Campbell. Caught in the act of trying to kill one of my own men, visions of a court-martial—of the loss of my commission—swam before me, as with one despairing effort I wrenched the blade out of the buckler, and, dropping its point to the Chief, stammered out my defence. "I really couldn't help it, Sir? He was showing the white feather. I was afraid he would bolt." To my intense relief the grim features relaxed into a smile." "Never mind," said Sir Colin, "you were quite right. They are trying to carry off some of their guns to the right front. Gallop after them and catch them." It may be imagined I lost no time in carrying out that order and placing as great a distance as possible between me and His Excellency. My young recruit came too, and afterwards behaved very well. He turned out a good soldier after that "baptism of fire."

A hard gallop soon brought us up with the flying enemy, who were "pounded" by a big ditch, where they abandoned the guns and took to their heels, but too late to save themselves. Here I had rather a narrow escape from abruptly ending my military experiences. Two "Pandies," whom I was pursuing, suddenly turned round and stood at bay, and almost simultaneously lashed at me with their *tulwars* as I charged between them. The man on the right brought his sword down on my head, fortunately protected by a thick "puggari," many folds of which it divided, and then glanced down on to my horse's shoulder, inflicting a long and deep wound. At the same moment I delivered a swinging cut on his own cranium which was covered by a small skull cup. That settled him effectually; but I had barely time to throw my sword round and receive on it a sweeping blow from the fellow on my left, which partially overpowered my guard and landed on my ribs, luckily much diminished in force; so that I escaped with a trifling flesh wound. He did not get another chance; for I dropped the point of my blade and ran him through the body. I was well out of that scrimmage, but my unlucky horse was quite disabled; so I had to dismount and entrust him to the care of one of my men, whose animal I borrowed for the rest of the day; and a very poor exchange I found it, both as regards charger and saddle.

I feel I must interrupt my narrative to beg the reader's indulgence for the introduction of descriptions of some of the adventures which happened to me personally. I trust he may believe that it is not due to any foolish desire to pose before him; nor to a wish, in the words of Mr. Wardle's fat boy, "to make his flesh creep;" but simply because I want to make these sketches as graphic as I can; and it seems to me that the effect would be to wash the colour out of them if I were to divest them of every touch of personal interest. In campaigns like those of the Mutiny in which our irregular cavalry was so freely used and played so important a part, hand-to-hand conflict was much more frequent than in ordinary wars. In fact, every officer of that branch had numberless opportunities of testing his skill at arms; for skirmishes were often of almost daily occurrence; and in each skirmish he carried his life literally at the point of his sword. To resume: A few minutes afterwards another adventure of a "touch and go" nature befell me. In a *mêlée* a brother officer had singled out a rebel foot soldier, and was hotly striving to cut him down, but his antagonist with bayonet fixed kept him at bay, and had just brought his musket to his shoulder to fire, when most luckily in the very nick of time I saw what was going on, and charged the Pandy, who, disconcerted by the sudden attack, hurriedly attempted to shift his aim on to me, but ineffectually. As he pulled the trigger his bullet sped harmlessly past my face, while I brought the edge of my sword down on his skull with such good will that it clave in two, and he fell dead. That fortunate interference in an unequally matched *combat à deux* probably saved from an untimely ending a life which has since proved of the highest value and usefulness, while it preserved to me a dear comrade and life-long friend. Among the most cherished of my possessions is the sword which he gave me as a memento of the affair.

The resistance offered by the enemy to Sir Colin's advance was not sufficiently serious to check it; and in fact no deployment of his troops was necessary. The heads of his columns steadily moved forward and gradually approached the position on the high ground which he had decided to occupy as affording the best point from which to carry out his plans for the subjugation of Lucknow.

While my troop was moving up a slope close to the Dilkhoosha we were suddenly gratified by the sight of a body of horse, about forty or fifty strong, which appeared in line on the crest of it coming towards us at a walk. The French-grey uniforms of this squad left no doubt as to its belonging to one of the old regular regiments; and my hopes rose high that now we were to have an opportunity of wiping out some of the disgrace which their treason had brought upon all who had belonged to their branch of the service of Old John Company: but the cowards declined to give us the chance.

"Threes about" they went the moment they saw us, and immediately disappeared, hidden from us by the rising ground. It may be imagined that we lost no time in driving in our spurs and galloping after them: but when we arrived at the top of the slope they had made such good use of their horses' legs that they were already far away, pelting along, in clouds of dust, over the plain below, and heading for a ford across the Goomti river, into which they presently plunged. The hurry they were in was good to see, as was their complete indifference to any pretence at keeping any sort of formation. Evidently they realised that this was no time to be hampered by pedantic adherence to "drill." Such mechanical regularity of movement might be all very well for the parade-ground; but in real soldiering, such as this, "individual initiative" must take its place. In they went, by twos and threes, just as they came to the ford, and floundered across: but at this juncture a couple of guns of ours opened on them, and made their passage very uncomfortable; for those who were not knocked out of their saddles got drenched by the splash of the projectiles. Once across, they continued their career at best speed for another mile or two before drawing rein. On the whole, I do not think they enjoyed that morning's ride very much.

VIII.

LUCKNOW.

A STORY is told of the behaviour of a company of Native Infantry on the establishment of a sister Presidency, which I may be pardoned for reproducing here, since it may be new to some of my readers.

The company in question was performing an uncommonly rapid movement to the rear, to get away from an undesirable neighbourhood, when a British officer, who tried to stop the stampede, roared after it Halt! Halt! Halt! At this a fat old Subadar, who was doing his best to keep up with his command, indignantly spluttered out as he scuttled along, puffing and blowing—"Kaun guddha halt bolta hai? Yih halt ka wakt nahin hai!" "What ass says halt! This is no time to halt." Down in Madras that story, if known, is doubtless put to the credit of a Bengal regiment, and probably with equal truth. *Si non e vero e ben trovato*—which must be my excuse for repeating it.

During this morning's work I happened to come across a British soldier—I think of the 9th Lancers—who had been wounded, but not very seriously, though sufficiently to cripple him. He was lying patiently under a tree waiting for the hospital establishment to come up and find him; and when I asked if I could do anything for him, he said he was suffering agonies from thirst, and would give anything for a drink of water. "Would you prefer beer?" I asked. "Oh, Sir," he replied, "don't make game of me." His face was delightful to see when I lugged out of one of my holsters a pint bottle of "Bass" which I had stowed in it according to my invariable practice, and knocked off its head by sliding my sword against it. The grateful fellow tried hard to make me drink half of it; but I could not resist the temptation of watching him swallow it to the last drop. When I presented him with a better Manilla cheroot than he had probably ever smoked in his life before, he began, I really believe, to think he was dreaming, and that such strange luck could not be real.

Before the evening of the next day a huge canvas city had sprung up in rear of the Dilkhoosha Palace. "The Cabul scale equipment" had not been invented in those days; and even subalterns luxuriated in large, old-fashioned hill tents, ten or twelve feet square, while the British soldiers were lodged in roomy-double-poled affairs; so that an encampment took up a deal more room than would now be required. No wonder that Sir Colin's army of fighting men was hampered by a much larger one of helpless camp-followers, of which Dr. Russell, the famous war correspondent, thus wrote:—"Who really can bring before his mind's eye a train of baggage animals twenty-five miles long, a string of sixteen thousand camels, a siege-train park covering a space of four hundred by four hundred yards, with twelve thousand oxen attached to it, and a following of sixty thousand non-combatants."

Sir Colin Campbell lost no time in pushing on the siege, for it practically began on the 2nd March, the day that he reached the Dilkhoosha. I well remember watching with admiration the brilliant performance of the Naval Brigade, the blue jackets of the *Shannon*, under the heroic Captain Peel, as they pushed forward to a position in front of the Palace, where, on the open ground sloping downwards towards the Martinière, without a vestige of cover, they planted their guns, and commenced a fierce reply to the cannonade of the rebels from the huge defensive earthworks which they had thrown up on the south-east of the City. Our gallant old Chief was far too wise, however, to throw his whole weight against these terrible lines of defence till he had discounted their value by the simple yet effective device of a turning movement, that old-established favourite with all great commanders. To carry out this design Sir

James Outram was sent across the Goomti, near Bibiapore, on the 6th of March, with a very strong force of all arms, which fought its way up the left bank of the river, driving the enemy before it, till, on the 9th, it had reached a position whence it successfully enfiladed the rebel lines of defence.

Now was Sir Colin able to advance without the enormous sacrifice of life which otherwise would have been inevitable. That day the Black Watch stormed the Martinière at the point of the bayonet without firing a shot. The day after, "Banks' House" was seized and promptly fortified; and from this coign of vantage, step by step, deliberately and irresistibly, did our Engineers and Artillery sap and breach the way for our infantry through block after block of buildings, till by the 21st of March every palace, mosque and walled enclosure in Lucknow had been carried, and the entire City was in our hands.

While this was being accomplished, my regiment had formed part of a Bri-

LA MARTINIERE, LUCKNOW.

gade under Brigadier W. Campbell, which marched round the City, past the Alumbagh, to a position opposite the Moosabagh, with the view of cutting off the escape of the rebels when they should be driven out of the town by the bayonets of the Infantry. During this movement we met with desultory opposition, and lost several lives; but we came across no large masses of the enemy; and there can be no doubt that thousands of them slipped through our fingers and effected their escape, to re-unite later on and prolong into the rapidly approaching "hot weather" a struggle which, if we had been more fortunate, would have been ended there and then. At the same time, in justice to Brigadier Campbell, it must be remembered that the semi-circle traversed by him was of great extent—probably more than thirty miles—and it needs no great effort of imagination to conceive how difficult was the task of preventing, with a small Brigade of Cavalry and Horse Artillery, so long a line from being penetrated by bodies of fugitives at one point or another, even by day, still more under cover of night.

I was much struck during this march by an instance of heroism on the part of two village matchlockmen which deserves record, and which, if it had been performed by natives of a European country in defence of their homes, would have been sung by poets in patriotic ballads, and would have earned for the brave actors an immortality of applause.

The scouts of the advanced guard were approaching a very broad deep "nullah" which I had been ordered to reconnoitre with the view of finding a practicable way across it for our guns. On the level plain behind us, under the bright sun, moved slowly onwards the strong body of Cavalry, of which we were merely the forerunners. Beyond the "nullah," nestled among its fields and mango groves a small village, from which emerged two tall peasants, clad in their usual white cotton working clothes, each of them carrying a matchlock.

With the utmost deliberation these two men approached the ravine, and, lying down in a sheltered hollow, opened fire on us. They could have been under no illusions as to their chances of escape. They saw that they were two against two thousand. They knew that their puny effort to stop us was hopeless; but yet they did all they could, and devoted themselves to death in defence of the brown mud walls which held their household gods. In vain we shouted to them that we did not intend to harm their village—that we were going past it, and would not enter it. They evidently did not believe us; and continued to load and fire with as much expedition as their long, clumsy, tinder-locks allowed them. They were sure to hit some of us in time: so we were obliged to scatter and cross the nullah at different points, and "fall upon them with the edge of the sword."

When the final great eruption of the rebels from the Moosabagh took place on the 21st March, Brigadier

Campbell was undoubtedly caught napping. It was not till many thousands of the enemy had streamed out and had already crossed miles of country that the Brigade was slipped in pursuit. The first to get under way were two troops of the 1st Sikh Irregulars under Captain the Hon'ble Hugh Chichester, with whom Lieutenant Sandeman and I were sent. We galloped for several miles without coming across more than a few scattered groups, and were beginning to think that the reported flight of the "Pandies" was a false alarm, when suddenly the numbers of the fugitives began to increase, and presently we were in the thick of them. With the exception of a few men of rank on elephants, they were all on foot. Their horsemen had got clean away from us. Our progress now became less rapid, for we were engaged in a series of "scrimmages," and before long the rest of the regiment came up, as did the 7th Hussars and the Military Train.

Late as we were in catching up the rebels, we yet inflicted great slaughter on them, with hardly any damage to ourselves till late in the day, almost at the end of the pursuit, when our regiment suffered an irreparable loss, which will be presently narrated.

We had, as usual in similar affairs, got broken up into small groups and single individuals, when I noticed on my left front a sturdy rascal, seemingly, from his dress, a dismounted cavalry soldier, stalking along, with a musket on his shoulder, sullenly disdaining to run. Him I marked for my prey and dashed after: but when I got within a few yards of him he faced about and covered me with his musket, expressing himself at the same time in very forcible terms of abuse and defiance. This uncompromising attitude on his part made me think it would be more prudent to shoot than to attempt to sabre him: so I wheeled off to the left and circled round him to the right, returned my sword, and drew my revolver. All this time he held his ground, slowly turning on his pivot, and never ceasing to follow my movements with his aim; but he reserved his fire, for no doubt he coolly reflected that, if he missed me, he would be at my mercy. Every barrel of my revolver did I empty at him, and every time without hitting him. Between his legs—under his arms—past his head—flew my bullets, till the whole six were expended. Nothing remained but to gallop away to a safe distance, re-load, and renew the experiment, or else to trust to my sword and charge him. I dare say that if there had been no witnesses about I would have chosen the former alternative: but there were many men of the regiment close by, and sheer shame prevented me; so I returned the useless pistol, drew my sword, and with my heart in my mouth went straight at him at full speed. As I raised my arm to smite, he pulled the trigger. Bending myself half out of the saddle on the near side I escaped the bullet, and delivered on his head with all my force a cut which dropped him to the ground. Though mortally wounded he was not dead; and he fumbled in his *cummerbund* for a revolver which was sticking out of it; so I dismounted, and as he—dazed and blinded—pulled the pistol out of his waist-cloth, I seized his wrist and directed his aim harmlessly into the air. I then wrenched the weapon from his grasp and used another barrel of it to put him out of his pain. That revolver was subsequently identified as having belonged to an officer named Thackwell, if my memory serves me right, who had been killed in the City a few days previously when separated from his comrades.

Some little time after this incident I saw a small group of fugitives far away on our left, making for a walled village, and it occurred to me to try a long shot at them with my Lancaster rifle, which was always carried by my orderly on a belt slung over his shoulder; so I turned round and asked for it, but the orderly was not to be seen, and some of the other men said:—"Don't you know, Sahib, that your orderly has been killed?" "Killed!" I exclaimed. "When? Has he not been following me all along?"

Then, for the first time, I learned that the faithful fellow, who must have been close at my heels when I charged the sepoy, but of whose presence in my excitement I had been totally oblivious, had been hit in the chest by the bullet which I had so narrowly escaped and had been seen to fall. I could not then return to the fatal spot, but I sent a couple of men back at once to find the poor fellow, and, if he should be still alive, to get a doolie and carry him to the hospital tent in camp.

For several miles we kept up the pursuit till we had apparently exhausted the lead—to use a miner's term—on which we had struck. We were about to give up the chase, when, from the far side of a ravine, a solitary fugitive fired his musket at a group of our officers. He must have aimed at the one who, from his full brown beard and apparent age, seemed to him the most important and most likely to be the commander. That shot cost us the life of our brave Commanding Officer. The gallant Captain Wale fell, mortally wounded by two slugs, one of which passed through his beard into his throat, the other into his mouth. He was instantly avenged, for, as the rebel sepoy turned to fly, he also fell dead, hit in the spine by a bullet from the revolver of Captain Chichester.

In a few minutes, to the deep grief of his officers and men, by whom he was loved as few Commanding Officers are ever loved, poor Wale breathed his last. A doolie was sent for from the rear, his body placed in it and reverently carried back to camp. Sick at heart, I now sought the place where my unfortunate orderly had met his fate. My worst fears were realized. He was dead. His body had not been disturbed by the men whom I had sent to find him, and he was lying on his back, the rifle underneath him, with a hole through the leather sling just where it crossed over the heart. Close by lay the corpse of the sepoy.

Very sad was our return to camp that day. I had no sooner placed before my tent the doolie in which was the body of my poor orderly than his father, a fine old Sikh, who also was a sowar in the regiment, and who, having remained in camp on that occasion, was in complete ignorance of our losses, came up to me with a smile on his handsome old face to ask after his son. My heart was too full to speak. I could only point to the doolie, the curtains of which were closed. Lifting one of them up, he looked in and knew his bereavement. The proud old soldier set his face hard, drew himself up, saluted me, and said :—" My son's 'nokri' (service) is over. Let me take his place. I will be your orderly now, Sahib." I am not ashamed to say that this touching act of simple, unaffected Spartan fortitude completely unmanned me.

The remains of the brave Captain Wale rest in the Moosabagh, a walled garden which formerly belonged to the Nawabs of Oudh, but which was confiscated from Wajid Ali, the last of that race, by the British Government. The massive walls and towers and gateways of the erst Royal pleasance are now rapidly crumbling into ruins. The huge garden which once bloomed within them is now a wilderness of thorns and jungle trees, interspersed with ill-kept patches of cultivation. Everything speaks of decay and neglect, except the tomb itself and its little walled enclosure, which I was glad to find on the 4th of January, 1891 in perfect repair, and shewing evident signs of careful attention on the part of the district authorities. About a furlong beyond the fourth milestone on the Lucknow-Bareilly road, and about a mile to the right, is the Moosabagh, in which, under the spreading arms of a fine old mango tree, will be found the solitary tomb, bearing on it the following inscription :—

"Sacred to the memory of Captain F. Wale, who raised and commanded the 1st Sikh Irregular Cavalry. Killed in action at Lucknow on the 1st March, 1858. This monument is erected by Captain L. B. Jones, Acting Commandant of the 1st Sikh Irregular Cavalry, as a token of regard for this officer, whom he admired both as a friend and soldier. Captain Wale lived and died a Christian Soldier."

The original designation of the 1st Sikh Irregular Cavalry has disappeared from the *Army List.* It is now known as the 11th (Prince of Wales' Own) Bengal Lancers. While that distinguished regiment continues to exist—and may that be as long as the British Empire itself!—will be imperishably associated with its annals the first name inscribed on its muster-roll, that of its Founder and first Commander, the gallant Captain Wale.

IX.

A HERO'S DEATH.

NOT long after following to the grave the remains of my beloved Commanding Officer, I was so unfortunate as to be prostrated by a severe attack of remittent fever, and to be sent on six months' sick leave to the hills.

Before closing these brief memoirs I must fulfil my promise of relating how my dear comrade and former Commanding Officer, Captain Sanford, lost his life.

He had succeeded the gallant Younghusband, who had been killed shortly before at Futtehgarh, in the command of a detachment of the 5th Punjab Cavalry, which formed part of the Mounted Brigade under Sir Hope Grant, and was attached to Sir James Outram's force during the operations in March, 1858 on the left bank of the Goomti. On the 10th of March, while the Cavalry Brigade was returning from a reconnaissance, it was fired on by a small group of rebels. Sir Hope Grant ordered Captain Sanford to attack these men; but before he could overtake them they had reached the shelter of a village which Sanford decided to reconnoitre personally before taking his men into it. He therefore dismounted them and left them outside, while he penetrated into the place without a single companion. He climbed on to the flat roof of a house, and moved forward to a low wall which separated it from the roof of the next house. Over that wall he must have vaulted, when he found himself confronted by the loopholes of a higher building within a few yards of him. From these loopholes a volley flashed, and he fell, struck by a bullet in the forehead. Thus ended a life which till that moment had seemed a charmed one. Always utterly reckless of his own safety, while considerate of others to a fault—a magnificent horseman—a finished master of swordsmanship--he had hitherto triumphantly and gaily carried his life through a hundred perils. His first wound was his last. The day before he fell he had read in the *Gazette* the announcement of his promotion to a brevet majority for distinguished service before Delhi: and doubtless his heart was full of soldierly pride and of hope of yet more brilliant honour when the fatal bullet suddenly and for ever stilled it.

As he did not return, the worst was feared; and a gallant young officer volunteered to go in search of him. With him went two of Sanford's men. They followed the route which he had taken, but had no sooner got on to the top of the house than another volley laid low both the sowars, killing one and wounding the other. The officer immediately dragged the wounded man off the house, and then returned and brought away the body of his comrade. Once more he started on his heroic errand, accompanied by two fresh volunteers. During the previous brief episode he had noticed that the loopholes in the high building were so cut that the muzzles of the muskets of its occupants could not be depressed at a very acute angle. He now left his two men at the foot of the wall of the house, and himself climbed on to the roof. Throwing himself flat on his stomach, he crawled up to the low partition-wall beyond which lay Captain Sanford's body. As he vaulted over this and again threw himself flat, a volley was fired, but missed him. His surmise proved to have been correct. While he lay prone the muskets of the rebels could not be depressed so as to hit him: so he crept up to the body, and, dragging it with him, reached the low wall. Exerting all his strength, he hoisted it over, and fell with it on the other side, escaping unscathed from the hurried fusillade which pursued him. In a few seconds he was once more in safety with his sacred burden. Then ensued a smart little fight. The village was stormed, and every one of the rebels in it was killed. The young hero whose story I have told was recommended by Sir Hope Grant for the Victoria Cross, which I have no doubt my readers will agree with me in thinking he had well earned, but— it was not awarded to him.

Though I was not an eye-witness of the events above described, and cannot therefore vouch from personal knowledge for the strict accuracy of all the details, the reader may perfectly rely on the main correctness of the relation: for I have repeated it as it was told to me at the time; and, deeply interested as I was in all that pertained to the fate of so dear a friend as was Sanford to me, the story burnt itself into my memory. Moreover, I have lately sought and obtained satisfactory confirmation of it.

About a hundred and fifty yards to the right of the Lucknow-Fyzabad road, and about a hundred yards beyond the bridge where that road crosses the Gokral nullah, stands an obelisk in a small walled enclosure. On a white marble tablet let in to the obelisk is the following inscription :—"Beneath this monument rest the mortal remains of Charles

Sanford, late Captain of the 3rd Bengal Light Cavalry, who, when gallantly leading a body of dismounted Punjab Cavalry in an assault on a fortified place near Lucknow, on the 10th March, 1858, met a soldier's death."

"Stranger: Respect the lonely resting-place of the brave!"

A slab on the wall of the enclosure records that it was consecrated by the Right Reverend Ralph, Bishop of Calcutta, on the 17th of January, 1878.

Truely, a lonely resting-place for the ashes of a hero. A solitary tree marks the spot on the bare brown plain, the desolate surface of which is scored by small ravines trending down to the Gokral nullah. Not far off is a village, probably the one where the gallant Sanford fell. A broad cultivated valley, through which the tortuous Goomti river rolls, like a huge snake, its sluggish folds, fills, to the south, the foreground of the landscape. Beyond the fields, through the distant haze, rise, embosomed among groves of trees, the domes and minarets of Lucknow—a beautiful and placid scene— realising the Poet's vision of a "haunt of ancient peace."

Such are now the surroundings of the sacred spot where, nearly thirty-three years ago, was laid to rest, while the air was thick with the smoke of battle, all that could die of the heroic Charles Sanford.

NOTE.

At the moment when Captain Wale was shot I had not yet rejoined him from the encounter related on page 197. I arrived on the spot just before he breathed his last. In the nullah, from the opposite bank of which Wale fired the fatal slugs, had been a number of fugitives, all of whom were destroyed.

In the skirmish with them was severely wounded the late Sir Robert Groves Sandeman, whose recent sudden death has deprived the Empire of one of its foremost and most devoted servants, and all who knew him of a loved and loyal friend.

So recently as on the 30th December last (1891), Sir Robert wrote me the following account of the fight in the nullah:—"I was with Wale at the time he "was shot, and when his orderly Gowrie "Shunker was also killed. There was "also an old Sikh with us who fought "right well and hard. I was twice "wounded with sword cuts—one cut on "my leg and the other on my arm. My "horse was also very badly wounded. "Wale was shot on the bank of a nullah, "and we had to get at the fellows in the "nullah and have a regular hand-to-hand "fight. The old Sikh who was with me is "now, I think, an A.-D.-C. to the Chief, "but of this I am not sure. After this "fight I was just able to crawl back to "poor old Wale, who was then breathing. "I then got help, and took, or rather was "carried in a doolie along with the "body (in another doolie) to camp."

INDEX.

THE END.